ART AT AUCTION 1978-79

JOHN SINGER SARGENT, RA
Portrait of Millicent, Duchess of Sutherland
Signed and dated *1904*, 100in by 57½in (254cm by 146cm)
New York $210,000 (£102,439). 7.VI.79
From the collection of the late Benjamin Sonnenberg

ART AT AUCTION

The Year at Sotheby Parke Bernet 1978-79

Two hundred and forty-fifth season

SOTHEBY PARKE BERNET

© Sotheby Parke Bernet Publications Ltd, 1979

First published for
Sotheby Parke Bernet Publications by
Philip Wilson Publishers Ltd,
Russell Chambers, Covent Garden, London WC2E 8AA
and
81 Adams Drive, Totowa, New Jersey 07512

Editor: Diana de Froment
Assistant editor: Joan A. Speers
Assistant: Betsy Pinover (USA)
Production: Peter Ling, Harry Tyler, Mary Osborne
Jacket photograph: Anthony Dawton

ISBN: 0 85667 063 4
ISSN: 0084–6783

Printed in England by Jolly & Barber Ltd, Rugby

The publishers would like to acknowledge the following for their
kind permission to reproduce illustrations:
Steven Tucker, New York, pp 8, 10, 11, 12
Galerie Welz, Salzburg, pp 110, 112, 114
The Colman Collection of Silver Mustard Pots, p 397

Endpaper illustration: A repeating pattern of part of the woodcut
border on the title page of *Pergaeus* by Apollonius translated from
Greek into Latin by Joannes Baptista Memus, Bernardino Bindoni,
Venice, 1537. This book is from the Honeyman Collection and was
sold in London on 30 October 1978 for £550($1,128)

Contents

A Luba wood stool by the 'Master of Buli', Zaire, height $22\frac{7}{8}$ in (58cm)
London £240,000 ($492,000). 21.VI.79

Note

Prices given throughout this book are the hammer prices exclusive of any buyer's premium or sales tax which may have been applicable in any of the salerooms. These prices are shown in the currency in which they were realised. The sterling and dollar equivalent figures, shown in brackets, are for guidance only and are based on the rounded rates of exchange on 31 May 1979. These rates, for each pound sterling, are as follows:

United States dollars, 2.05; Canadian dollars, 2.40; Hong Kong dollars, 10.50; French francs, 9.10; Swiss francs, 3.55; Dutch guilders, 4.30; Italian lire, 1,760; South African rand, 1.75; German marks, 3.95; Spanish pesetas, 136

Sotheby Parke Bernet's two main galleries, in Great Britain and the United States, are indicated by the designation 'London' or 'New York'. Additional salerooms in these two cities are referred to as 'Belgravia' and 'Hodgson's Rooms' (London) and 'PB Eighty-four' (New York)

The second-floor landing of Ben Sonnenberg's home at Number Nineteen Gramercy Park, New York.
In the foreground is an English eighteenth-century triple-back settee and on the walls is hung part of
his large collection of Old Master and Modern drawings

Possessed and possessing: shopping for 'bits' with Ben Sonnenberg

Brendan Gill

Benjamin Sonnenberg, invariably addressed as Ben, was the best-known public relations man in the United States up to the time of his death, in September 1978. He presided over what was surely the grandest house in New York City, Number Nineteen Gramercy Park, a red-brick Victorian mansion of some thirty-seven rooms, nearly all of them crammed with precious objects: eighteenth-century English and Irish furniture, Old Master drawings, paintings, Roman antiquities, brass in a score of different forms, china, silver and pewter. Number Nineteen was the work of art upon which he and his wife laboured contentedly for over fifty years and its hundreds of disparate treasures manifested a shrewd and playful eccentricity. To mingle them as he did was to make a gesture as personal as his signature, for he never sought to shoulder his way into history by dint of being a superb collector; he never wished a monument to the cleverness of his eye and the timely opening of his purse. For years, he earned his living feeding the vanity of other men and afterward struggling to keep that vanity within bounds, and he feared being thought to be one of their puffed-up company. If it amused him to cause a certain noise in the world, he was under no misapprehension as to how he had accomplished it, and why. He made himself conspicuous in order to become, when he chose to do so, invisible.

The one occasion in his life when he might have consented to be the centre of attention was the opening a few years ago, at the Pierpont Morgan Library, of an exhibition of drawings from his collection. The director of the Library, Charles Ryskamp, waited hour after hour for Ben to take his rightful place beside him. In vain; Ben was in hiding elsewhere. For once, he had misjudged a situation. He was making sure of something wholly unnecessary: that the guests of the Library did not assume from his presence that he was unaware of the distance lying between him and the objects he was fortunate enough to have temporarily in his possession.

More than most men I know, Ben seemed in age to be increasingly at ease with the temporary. He found it droll that some of his associates expected their wealth to serve as a dispensation from ever having to die; so far, he said, the evidence was against them. (Here Ben would lean back and laugh, with the glee of a schoolboy who has learned something of value sooner than his comrades.) He had been a possessed collector, and little harm and much pleasure had come of it, but possession in the other sense – in the sense of permanent ownership – was a concept as implausible as

Peter Wilson, the Chairman, auctions the *Portrait of Mrs Joshua Montgomery Sears* by John Singer
Sargent in the main gallery in Madison Avenue. To the right is John Marion, the President of Sotheby
Parke Bernet Inc, standing next to Sargent's *Portrait of Millicent, Duchess of Sutherland*

the outwitting of death. 'I won't be here always,' Ben would say to me, in exactly the
same cheerful tone of voice that he would use in regretting an invitation to lunch, 'I'm
no good for you Friday.' He looked with equanimity upon the eventual scattering of
his collection; that this was bound to happen sooner or later did not prevent him from
adding to it whenever something charming caught his fancy. Within a few weeks of
his death he bought a self-portrait by a nineteenth-century French artist named
Achille Laugé. Characteristically, Ben was attracted to the picture by reason of an
oddity; in the margin of the drawing, Laugé had tested his charcoals with a few
practice squiggles.

It is because Ben felt as he did about the dispersal of his treasures that I speak with
confidence of the success of the auction, not in terms of money alone but in terms of
emotion as well. Like most old friends of Ben's, I had wondered whether those five
busy June days at Sotheby Parke Bernet would prove to be a harrowing occasion. Not
so, for nothing that happened during the auction was contrary to Ben's wishes, or
contrary to Ben's hopes. Lot after lot was brought out, bid on, and knocked down at a
handsome price, often enough to a friend of the family. Ben was in the habit of calling

his older friends 'cronies' and his younger friends 'rascals', and a reassuring assortment of cronies and rascals was present daily in the auction room. As for the auctioneers, beginning with Peter Wilson, they were men whom Ben admired and had often bought from in the past. And so he was always intensely among us, both through memory and through the objects themselves, as they came up for sale.

Again and again in the course of the auction, I would recognise some piece that Ben had picked up during a long day's stroll through the streets of London, Paris, Dublin, or any of a dozen other cities. Tagging along as he gazed and judged, I would marvel at the art of shopping as he had perfected it – an art that had blessedly little to do with cash, or travellers' cheques, or the usual means of identification. Having hit upon something that pleased him and having scarcely seemed to hear its price, he would say to the stranger waiting upon him, 'Send that, if you will, to Nineteen Gramercy Park, in New York.' And the stranger would bow and say without hesitation, 'Very good, Mr Sonnenberg. Thank you very much.'

I in the street afterward, incredulously: 'But how on earth – ?'

Ben: 'It must be my moustache.'

The William and Mary room, showing some of Ben Sonnenberg's fine pieces of English furniture and decorations and, to the left, the bust of *Diego* by Alberto Giacometti

The ballroom, featuring the William IV breakfront bookcase. To the far left can be seen the George III
rent table, and on the right is *Portrait of a woman* by William Merritt Chase

In conversation, if someone were to praise Ben's collection to his face, he would
take care to minimise its importance by saying that it consisted of 'bits', or 'scraps',
or even 'keepsakes'. Some of these keepsakes might be grander than others – the
George III mahogany rent table, for example, or the William IV breakfront – but the
word had a ring of true feeling within its playfulness. For they *were* keepsakes; Ben
cherished them. Among the antiquities that sold well at the auction were several that I
remember his buying one afternoon in Lugano, just ten years ago. What a happy day
that turned out to be for him, after what a sorry start! We had been travelling through
Switzerland, and to his dismay Ben had yet to find a single 'bit' that interested him. As
we drove down into Lugano, only a few hours remained before we had to set out for
home. In something like despair, Ben said, 'But I've never *been* in a country where I
didn't buy *some*thing!' His face was pale; he appeared inconsolable. A moment later,
he caught sight of the shop of Pino Donati. In the window was an ancient Roman
marble lion's head, splendidly baleful. There were plenty of other lion's heads back
at Number Nineteen, in brass and silver and the Lord knew what, but there was no
such thing as a man's having too many lions' heads. I saw the colour coming back into
Ben's cheeks. His black eyes were merry. 'My dear boy,' he said, 'let's go in and take
a little look around.'

For illustrations of individual objects see frontispiece and appropriate sections

Paintings and Drawings

PSEUDO-PIER FRANCESCO FIORENTINO
The Madonna and Child
On panel, late fifteenth century, $23\frac{1}{2}$in by $17\frac{1}{2}$in (59.6cm by 44.5cm)
London £60,000 ($123,000). 11.VII.79
Formerly in the collection of the late Adolphe Stoclet

MARIOTTO DI NARDO
The Madonna and Child enthroned with Saints
On panel, *circa* 1394 – 1424, 37in by 25¼in (94cm by 64cm)
London £40,000 ($82,000). 1.XI.78

LORENZO DI BICCI
The Madonna and Child with Saints
On panel, *circa* 1370–1427, 46¼in by 27in (117.5cm by 68.5cm)
London £40,000 ($82,000). 1.XI.78

THE MASTER OF SAN GAGGIO
A triptych: The Madonna and Child with Saints and scenes from the Passion
On panel, fourteenth century, 18½in by 25½in (47cm by 64.7cm)
London £25,000 ($51,250). 13. XII.78

JACOBELLO DEL FIORE
The Madonna of Humility
On panel, early fifteenth century, 11¾in by 18½in (29cm by 47cm)
London £38,000 ($77,900). 1.XI.78

Attributed to FERNANDO GALLEGO
Christ on the road to Calvary
On panel, late fifteenth century, 61¾in by 78¾in (157cm by 200cm)
El Quexigal Ptas 3,500,000 (£25,735:$52,757). 25.V.79
From the collection of the Hohenlohe family

ALTOBELLO MELONE
Portrait of a young man
On panel, 1497 – 1517, 27¾in by 22¼in (70.5cm by 56.5cm)
London £43,000 ($88,150). 1.XI.78

JAN BRUEGHEL THE ELDER
A still life of flowers
On copper, early seventeenth century, 13¾in by 10½in (35cm by 26.5cm)
New York $410,000 (£200,000). 12.I.79

A still life by Jan Brueghel the Elder

Brenda Auslander

When Napoleon's brother, Joseph Bonaparte, was forced to abdicate as King of Spain in 1813, he fled to the United States under the assumed name Comte de Survilliers, and settled in Bordentown, New Jersey. He took with him a collection of Old Master paintings, probably formed during his years in Italy and Spain, which was one of the very few known to have existed in the early decades of the new American Republic.

The year after his death in 1844 a sale of 'paintings and statuary' was held at his estate arousing considerable public notice and curiosity. Among the 128 lots listed in the catalogue were seven paintings by Claude-Joseph Vernet (several of which were acquired by the Pennsylvania Academy of Fine Arts), a still life by Cornelis de Heem, a collaborative work by Peter Paul Rubens and Frans Snyders, and a small picture by Jan van Os (1744–1808). The painting by van Os, purchased by an anonymous buyer, disappeared until 26 April 1912 when it resurfaced as lot 187 in a sale in New York organised by the American Art Association. It was bought by a private New York collector and was later inherited by his son.

When this still life came to public auction for the third time, last January, it was newly ascribed to Jan Brueghel the Elder (1568–1625). Today it is difficult to understand how Brueghel's style could be confused with that of a painter active almost two centuries later. Connoisseurship frequently runs parallel to taste and perhaps the early nineteenth-century vogue for works by van Os had sufficient strength to temper this mistaken attribution for over one hundred years.

The composition of an embossed tumbler on a table, filled with an assortment of periwinkles, roses, an iris, a tulip and a star of David, is typical of Brueghel's work (see opposite). His scientific approach and botanical precision are expressed not only in the flowers and glass but also in the carefully depicted insects. This introspective rendering is far from the opulent style and forceful compositions of van Os, who also used lighter backgrounds, in the tradition of van Huysum.

In 1977 when *Flowers in a wooden tub* was sold in Amsterdam[1] Brueghel's sudden popularity astonished the art world, and the following year a record price of almost twice the amount was realised by a similar painting, *Flowers in a glass beaker*.[2] The appearance on the art market of a third still life created special excitement not only because of these two precedents, but also because it was an undisputed and formerly unrecognised work.

[1] See *Art at Auction 1976–77*, p 41
[2] See *Art at Auction 1977–78*, p 31

ROELANDT SAVERY
A fantastic landscape, workers at a mine sifting for gold
On panel, signed and dated *1613*, $6\frac{7}{8}$in by $10\frac{5}{8}$in (17.5cm by 27cm)
New York $130,000(£63,415). 12.1.79

SALOMON VAN RUYSDAEL
The river Waal near Gorinchem
On panel, seventeenth century,
16¾in by 14½in (41.5cm by 37cm)
Amsterdam Fl 740,000 (£172,093:
$352,791). 7.XI.78

FRANS POST
Landscape with ruins and the
mission post of Olinda, Brazil
On panel, signed and dated *1662*,
13⅝in by 18½in (34.5cm by 47cm)
Amsterdam Fl 380,000 (£88,372:
$181,163). 7.XI.78

BALTHASAR VAN DER AST
A still life of flowers
On panel, signed, seventeenth century, 22¾in by 17¼in (57.7cm by 44cm)
New York $145,000(£70,732). 30.V.79

JAN DAVIDSZ. DE HEEM
A still life of flowers and fruit
Seventeenth century, 15¾in by 14¾in (40cm by 37.5cm)
London £65,000 ($133,250). 11.VII.79

MELCHIOR DE HONDECOETER
Ornamental birds in a park
Signed, seventeenth century, 67¾in by 102½in (172cm by 260.3cm)
London £45,000($92,250). 28.III.79
From the collection of Sir James Hutchison, DSO, LLD

PIETER BRUEGHEL THE YOUNGER
A wedding procession
On panel, signed and dated 1627, 29½in by 47¼in (75cm by 120cm)
London £90,000 ($184,500). 11.VII.79
From the collection of the Carrier family

ANTONIO CANALE called CANALETTO
Venice: the bacino di San Marco
23 in by 36½ in (58.5 cm by 92.7 cm)
London £120,000 ($246,000). 1.XI.78

FRANCOIS BOUCHER
Landscape with figures on a bridge by a tower
Signed, 32in by 56¼in (81.3cm by 143cm)
London £75,000 ($153,750). 1.XI.78

FRANCISCO JOSÉ DE GOYA Y LUCIENTES
Infante Don Luis de Borbón and the architect Don Ventura Rodríguez
Circa 1783, 10¼in by 7¾in (26cm by 19.5cm)
London £60,000 ($123,000). 28.III.79
From the collection of Claude Guerlain

CHARLES-ANDRE (CARLE) VAN LOO
Portrait of Giovanni Paolo Panini
Circa 1730, 38in by 30in (96.5cm by 76.2cm)
London £48,000 ($98,400). 28.III.79

CARLO MARATTA
Study for a figure of Africa
Red chalk, *circa* 1675, 17in by 12$\frac{3}{8}$in
(43.1cm by 31.5cm)
London £16,000 ($32,800). 7.XII.78
Now in the Los Angeles County
Museum, California

This drawing belongs to a series of
preparatory studies for frescoes in the
Grand Salone of the Palazzo Altieri, Rome

FRANCESCO PRIMATICCIO
Studies of a stooping figure and a woman
Red chalk heightened with white, *circa* 1552,
$8\frac{7}{8}$in by $7\frac{5}{8}$in (22.5cm by 19.2cm)
London £7,000 ($14,350). 28.VI.79

These figures are studies for a spandrel in the
ballroom of the Château de Fontainebleau

GIOVANNI BATTISTA CRESPI called IL CERANO
Two kneeling saints
Brown wash over black and red chalk
heightened with white on blue paper,
$11\frac{1}{2}$in by $9\frac{1}{8}$in (29.3cm by 23.2cm)
London £4,500 ($9,225). 28.VI.79

Now in the British Museum, London

FRANCESCO CURRADI
A young girl sleeping
Coloured chalk, $9\frac{1}{8}$in by $15\frac{7}{8}$in (23cm by 40.5cm)
London £5,800 ($11,890). 28.VI.79

GIOVANNI BATTISTA PIAZZETTA
Apollo and others praising Torquato Tasso
Black chalk, 16¾in by 11¼in
(42.5cm by 29.7cm)
London £8,800 ($18,040). 7.XII.78

BIAGIO PUPINI called DALLE LAME
Daedalus and Icarus
Pen and brown ink and wash heightened with
white on paper washed brown, 15in by 15⅜in
(38cm by 39.2cm)
London £4,200 ($8,610). 28.VI.79

JACOPO ZANGUIDI called IL BERTOJA
*Study for a circular composition of Joseph's
second dream*
Pen and brown ink and wash heightened
with white over traces of black chalk on
blue-grey paper, 9⅝in by 9⅜in
(24.4cm by 23.7cm)
London £4,200 ($8,610). 28.VI.79

A study for one of the frescoes of the Sala dei
Sogni in the Palazzo Farnese, Caprarola

PIERO BUONACCORSI called PERINO DEL VAGA
The raising of Lazarus
Pen and black ink and grey wash over black
chalk, 11¼in by 8⅛in (28.6cm by 20.7cm)
London £5,500 ($11,275). 28.VI.79

This is a preliminary study for the fresco
formerly in the Massimi Chapel, S. Trinità dei
Monti, Rome (*circa* 1538–40), and now in the
Victoria and Albert Museum, London

LORENZO TIEPOLO
A young boy resting his head on his hand
Red and black chalk, inscribed on the verso
Lorenzo Tiepolo/morto in spagnia, 15in by 11in
(38cm by 28cm)
London £7,200 ($14,760). 28.VI.79

FRANCISCO JOSÉ DE GOYA Y LUCIENTES
Gimiendo y llorando (weeping and wailing)
Black chalk, 7½in by 5⅞in (19.1cm by 15cm)
London £62,000 ($127,100). 28.VI.79

A sheet from an album of drawings which Goya
made in Bordeaux between 1824 and 1828

JACOPO ROBUSTI called **IL TINTORETTO**
A male nude figure reclining
Black chalk heightened with white on blue paper, 5⅝in by 10⅛in (14.2cm by 25.7cm)
London £7,200 ($14,760). 28.VI.79

ANNIBALE CARRACCI
Study of a boy lying on his back
Red chalk, 7¼in by 10¼in (18.6cm by 26cm)
London £16,000 ($32,800). 28.VI.79

This is one of three drawings representing the same boy, all of which can be dated *circa* 1585

JEAN HONORÉ FRAGONARD, after PETER PAUL RUBENS
The funeral of Decius Mus
Brush and brown wash and black chalk on cream paper, $9\frac{7}{8}$in by $14\frac{3}{8}$in (25cm by 36.5cm)
New York $21,000 (£10,244). 5.VI.79
From the collection of the late Benjamin Sonnenberg

This drawing was made after one of six paintings by Peter Paul Rubens, all executed *circa* 1618, of the story of the life of Consul Decius Mus. Fragonard's patron, Bergeret de Grancourt, records the artist's visit on 10 and 11 August 1774 to the Palais Lichtenstein, Vienna, where he would have seen Rubens' painting of this subject

ETIENNE–CHARLES LE GUAY
Jeune fille à la lecture
Red chalk and black crayon heightened with white, 15$\frac{7}{8}$in by 11$\frac{1}{4}$in (40.5cm by 28.7cm)
Monte Carlo FF 21,000 (£2,308:$4,731). 11.II.79

GEORGE LAMBERT
A classical landscape with ruined columns
57in by 47½in (145cm by 120.5cm)
London £20,000 ($41,000). 29.XI.78
From the collection of Gerald Hochschild

JAN SIBERECHTS
A view of Henley
Signed and dated *16--, 32¾in by 49¾in (83cm by 126.5cm)
London £90,000 ($184,500). 21.III.79

ARTHUR WILLIAM DEVIS
Weaving muslin
17¾in by 23½in (45cm by 60cm)
London £6,200 ($12,710). 21.III.79

This is one of a set of twenty-three paintings by Devis illustrating the Arts, Manufactures and
Agriculture of Bengal, sold for a total of £45,000 ($92,250)

GEORGE STUBBS, ARA
Newmarket Heath, with the rubbing-down house
Circa 1764–65, 12in by 16¼in (30.5cm by 41cm)
London £43,000 ($88,150). 18.VII.79

Now in the Tate Gallery, London

JOHN CONSTABLE, RA
Hampstead Heath – fine evening – wind N.W.
Inscribed with the title and dated *October 25, 1820,*
5½ in by 9⅝ in (14cm by 24.5cm)
London £25,000 ($51,250). 21.III.79
From the collection of Sir Geoffrey Keynes, FRCS

JOHANN HEINRICH FUSELI, RA
Martha Hess as Silence
Pencil, black and white chalk and bodycolour on buff paper, 1780–90, 22½in by 13in (57cm by 33cm)
London £21,000($43,050). 30.XI.78

THOMAS GAINSBOROUGH, RA
Portrait of Joshua Grigby of Drinkstone Park, Suffolk
$49\frac{1}{2}$in by $39\frac{3}{4}$in (125.5cm by 101cm)
London £76,000 ($155,800). 21.III.79

GEORGE CHINNERY
Portrait of William Prinsep and Mary his wife
Circa 1820, 35¼in by 27in (89.5cm by 68.5cm)
London £30,500 ($62,525). 21.III.79
From the collection of Colin James

WILLIAM SADLER II
A distant view of the Sugar Loaf, Co. Wicklow
On panel, 8¾in by 13in (22cm by 33cm)
Slane Castle £4,381 ($8,981). 26.VI.79

ERSKINE NICHOL, ARA, RSA
An ejected family
Signed and dated *1853*, 19½in by 32in (50cm by 82cm)
Slane Castle £13,000 ($26,650). 20.XI.78

THOMAS GAINSBOROUGH, RA
Wooded landscape with figures and country cart
Pencil and black chalk, watercolour and bodycolour, late 1760s, 9$\frac{1}{4}$in by 12$\frac{1}{4}$in (23.5cm by 31cm)
London £13,000 ($26,650). 22.III.79

JOSEPH MALLORD WILLIAM TURNER, RA
Florence from near San Miniato
Watercolour, *circa* 1828, 12½in by 19in (32cm by 48cm)
London £32,000 ($65,600). 19.VII.79

JOHN FREDERICK LEWIS, RA
Lord Ponsonby's horses held by grooms at Stamboul
Red and black chalk, watercolour and bodycolour on buff paper, *circa* 1840,
13½in by 19½in (34cm by 49.5cm)
London £32,000 ($65,600). 19.VII.79
From the collection of Mrs P. Ovenden

JOHN MARTIN
Joshua spying out the Land of Canaan
Watercolour and bodycolour, scraping out, and occasionally heightened with gum arabic, *circa* 1850,
14½in by 30in (37cm by 76cm)
London £20,000 ($41,000). 19.VII.79

ARTHUR HUGHES
A birthday picnic: portraits of the children of William and Anne Pattinson of Felling, near Gateshead
Signed, 1867, 39in by 50in (99cm by 127cm)
Belgravia £22,000 ($45,100). 24.X.78

This painting was exhibited at the Royal Academy in 1867. The scene is in Fellingwood, Northumberland, and depicts the fifth birthday party of Norman Percy Pattinson

SIR JOHN EVERETT MILLAIS, PRA
A Huguenot
On board, signed with monogram, *circa* 1855, 9¾in by 7in (25cm by 18cm)
Belgravia £33,000 ($67,650). 19.III.79

This is a reduced replica of *A Huguenot, on St Bartholomew's Day, refusing to shield himself from danger by wearing the Roman Catholic badge* painted by Millais in 1852, and exhibited at the Royal Academy with the following quotation from A. Marsh's *The Protestant Reformation in France*, 1847, 'When the clock of the Palais de Justice shall sound upon the great bell, at daybreak, then each good Catholic must bind a strip of white linen round his arm, and place a fair white cross in his cap.– The Order of the Duke of Guise'

DANTE GABRIEL ROSSETTI
Girl singing to a lute
Watercolour heightened with bodycolour,
signed and dated *1853*, 8¾in by 4in (22cm by 10cm)
Belgravia £8,200 ($16,810). 19.III.79

SIR EDWARD COLEY BURNE-JONES, ARA
Santa Dorothea
Coloured chalk, 1862, 67½in by 22in
(171.5cm by 56cm)
Belgravia £9,500 ($19,475). 24.X.78

This is one of the cartoons for the east
window of St Martin's Church,
Brampton, which was commissioned
by the artist's friend, George Howard,
9th Earl of Carlisle

SIR JOHN EVERETT MILLAIS, PRA
Esther, 'Now it came to pass on the third day that Esther put on her royal apparel and stood in the inner court of the king's house'
Signed with monogram, 1865, 41½in by 29½in (105.5cm by 75cm)
Belgravia £26,000 ($53,300). 19.III.79

The brocade worn by Esther belonged to General Gordon who wore it when he sat for his portrait by Valentine Prinsep. When Millais arranged the same robe on his sitter he decided to turn it inside out so as to obtain broader masses of colour and a more abstract effect. In 1865, when the painting was shown at the Royal Academy, *The Illustrated London News* noted, 'As a colour-study of three masses of yellow, blue and white it is . . . extremely beautiful, . . . and the whole is startlingly effective'

JOHN ATKINSON GRIMSHAW
Salthouse Docks, Liverpool
Signed, *circa* 1865, 23½in by 36in (60cm by 91.5cm)
Belgravia £20,000 ($41,000). 19.III.79

JACQUES JOSEPH TISSOT
Les adieux
Black chalk and grey wash heightened with white on buff paper, signed,
circa 1873, 39in by 24in (99cm by 61cm)
Belgravia £11,000 ($22,550). 24.X.78

An oil painting of this subject was exhibited at the Royal Academy in 1872,
and is now in the City Art Gallery, Bristol

EDWARD LEAR
Mount Tomohrit, Albania
'Tomohrit, Athos, all things fair,
With such a pencil, such a pen,
You shadow forth to distant men,
I read and felt that I was there'
                    A. Tennyson
Signed with monogram, *circa* 1848, 48in by 73in (122cm by 186cm)
Belgravia £45,000 ($92,250). 24.X.78

When Edward Lear was travelling in Albania he recorded in his journal this description which
corresponds almost exactly to the painting, '. . . but when the route began to ascend from the valley, the
view southward over to Skumbi, in which the giant Tomohr or Tomohrit, forms the one point of the
scene, was remarkably grand. . . . How glorious, in spite of the dimming scirocco haze, was the view
from the summit, as my eyes wandered over the perspective of winding valley and stream to the
farthest edge of the horizon – a scene realising the fondest fancies of artist imagination! The wide
branching oak, firmly riveted in crevices, all tangled over with fern and creepers, hung half-way down
the precipices of the giant crag, while silver-white goats (which chime so picturesquely in with such
landscapes as this) stood motionless as statues on the highest pinnacle, sharply defined against the clear
blue sky'. The verse quoted above is from Tennyson's poem, *To E. L., on his travels in Greece*, and is
inscribed on the mount

GEORGE HENRY, RA, RSA, ARSW
A promenade
Signed, 44½in by 22in (113cm by 56cm)
Gleneagles £10,000 ($20,500). 29.VIII.78

This painting was exhibited at the Royal Academy in 1912

ALFRED AUGUSTUS GLENDENING JR
Her Lady's pets
Watercolour heightened with white, signed with
monogram and dated *1902*, 20½in by 29in (52cm by 74cm)
Belgravia £2,200 ($4,510). 3.VII.79

MYLES BIRKET FOSTER, RWS
The footpath by the waterlane
Watercolour heightened with bodycolour,
signed with monogram, *circa* 1860, 31in by 26in
(79cm by 66cm)
Belgravia £5,000 ($10,250). 13.II.79

ELEANOR FORTESCUE BRICKDALE, RWS
'I did but see her passing by and yet I love her till I die'
Watercolour, signed with monogram, *circa* 1905,
13in by 10in (33cm by 25.4cm)
Belgravia £1,100 ($2,255). 19.III.79

FRANK DADD
Winter fun
Watercolour heightened with white, signed and dated *'93*,
14in by 19in (35.5cm by 48.2cm)
Belgravia £4,800 ($9,840). 3.VII.79

SIR WILLIAM ORPEN, RA, RHA
Reflection, a self-portrait
Circa 1910, 29½in by 24½in (75cm by 62.2cm)
Slane Castle £9,000 ($18,450). 20.XI.78
From the collection of Leonard P. Lee

CHARLES GINNER, ARA
The wet street, Dieppe
Signed, 1911, 23½in by 17½in (59.7cm by 44.5cm)
London £11,000 ($22,550). 27.VI.79

HAROLD GILMAN
Interior
Signed, *circa* 1915, 16¾in by 10¾in (42.5cm by 27.3cm)
London £19,000 ($38,950). 27.VI.79
From the collection of David Auchterlonie

EDWARD SEAGO
The quay at Honfleur
On board, signed, 26in by 36in (66cm by 91.5cm)
London £8,500 ($17,425). 27.VI.79

SIR ALFRED MUNNINGS, PRA
Major E. W. Shackle, Master
of the Buckinghamshire and
Berkshire Farmers' Hunt
Signed, $24\frac{1}{2}$in by $29\frac{1}{2}$in
(62.2cm by 75cm)
London £12,000 ($24,600).
27.VI.79

LAURENCE STEPHEN LOWRY, RA
The steps
Signed and dated *1940*, 20$\frac{1}{2}$in by 16$\frac{1}{2}$in (52cm by 42cm)
London £12,000 ($24,600). 15.XI.78
From the collection of N.D. Herbert

HENRY MOORE, OM, CH
Drawing for metal sculpture
Coloured chalk and watercolour, signed and dated '38, 15in by 21½in (38cm by 54.5cm)
London £6,800 ($13,940). 14.III.79

DAME BARBARA HEPWORTH
Two forms
Alabaster on a wooden base, 1949,
overall height 8¼in (21cm)
London £4,600 ($9,430). 14.III.79
From the collection of E.R.F. Cole

AUGUSTUS JOHN
Lady Ottoline Morrell
Gouache and pencil, signed, *circa* 1908, 14$\frac{3}{8}$in by 11$\frac{5}{8}$in (36.5cm by 29.5cm)
New York $19,000(£9,268). 9.VI.79
From the collection of the late Benjamin Sonnenberg

FERDINAND DE BRAEKELEER
Le ménage heureux
One of a pair, on panel, signed and dated *Antwerpen 1853*, 28½in by 22½in (72.4cm by 57.2cm)
New York $60,000 (£29,268). 3.V.79
From the collection of the Corcoran Gallery of Art, Washington DC

JOHANN BERNARD KLOMBEEK and EUGENE JOSEPH VERBOECKHOVEN
The trip to market
Signed by both artists and dated *1869*, 35in by 48¼in (89cm by 122.5cm)
London £20,000($41,000). 14.II.79

CHRISTIAN MALI
Peasant couple watering cattle and sheep
Signed and dated *München 1888*, 22in by 44½in (56cm by 113cm)
London £15,000($30,750). 22.XI.78

EUGENE ISABEY
L'Ecu de France
Signed and dated '57, 28in by 23in (71cm by 58.5cm)
London £11,000 ($22,550). 22.XI.78
From the collection of the late L. Martineau

JEAN RICHARD GOUBIE
The Paris Zoo
Signed and dated *1882*, 26¾in by 39¼in (68cm by 100cm)
New York $90,000 (£43,902). 13.X.78

EDGARD MAXENCE
Les fleurs du lac
Oil and tempera on panel, signed and dated *1900*, 34¼in by 61⅜in (87cm by 156cm)
London £15,000 ($30,750). 9.V.79

WILLIAM ADOLPHE BOUGUEREAU
Jeunes bohémiennes
Signed and dated *1879*, 65½in by 39in (166cm by 99cm)
New York $62,500(£30,488). 4.V.79

HENDRIK JOHANNES WEISSENBRUCH
Drawbridge over a canal
On panel, signed, $10\frac{1}{8}$in by $14\frac{1}{8}$in (25.7cm by 36cm)
Amsterdam Fl 80,000 (£18,605:$38,140). 7.XI.78

JEAN BERAUD
Le boulevard St Denis, Paris
Signed, 15¼in by 22in (38.5cm by 56cm)
New York $70,000 (£34,146). 26.I.79
From the collection of Louis H. Hollister

Fig 1
ALFRED STEVENS
Ready for the fancy-dress ball
Signed and dated *1879*, 35in by 45½in (89cm by 115.5cm)
New York $80,000 (£39,025). 13.X.78

Paintings from
William Vanderbilt's collection

Jerry E. Patterson

On Thursdays in New York in the 1880s respectable persons who had previously applied for a card were kindly admitted by Mr William Henry Vanderbilt to tour his private art gallery. The gallery, the finest in the country, occupied the entire rear ground floor of the Vanderbilt mansion at 640 Fifth Avenue, between 51st and 52nd Streets and had its own entrance, with Venetian mosaic foyer, on 51st Street. Vanderbilt, President of the New York Central Railroad and colossus of American transportation, whose fortune was estimated in 1880 at $200,000,000, built the enormous house, which the newspapers liked to call 'The Taj Mahal of New York', in 1881–82. Next door he built a house of similar size for his married daughters to share, so that the twin Vanderbilt mansions occupied an entire Fifth Avenue blockfront diagonally across from St Patrick's Cathedral and just north of today's Rockefeller Center. After seeing the houses and their sumptuous interiors one chronicler asserted that 'the Vanderbilts have come nobly forward and shown the world how millionaires ought to live'.

Visitors to the art gallery were seeing Vanderbilt's own particular favourite among the hundred or so rooms in the twin mansions, which also included 'Early English', 'Grecian', and 'Japanese' parlours. With thirty-five foot ceilings there was ample room in the gallery for the collection of paintings, hung on the red velvet walls one on top of the other as was the current fashion. The collection of over one hundred paintings had cost – no secret was made of the amount, quite the contrary – $1,500,000, spent between 1874 and the collector's death in 1885.

The paintings without exception were 'modern', meaning the works of contemporary artists. Legend seems to assert that nineteenth-century Americans when they became rich bought Rembrandts, but that was not a rule until the next generation. Vanderbilt and many of his friends were collectors of academic-realist paintings by living artists such as Gérôme, Detaille and Bonheur. The Paris Salon was the shrine of that school of painting and Vanderbilt often bought from its walls, visiting France himself four times between 1879 and 1884. Also, he often used as his agent, Samuel Putnam Avery, America's most prominent art dealer who made frequent buying trips to the major European exhibitions. The educated public shared Vanderbilt's taste and art critics thought that his gallery was 'an important element

Fig 2
JEAN LOUIS ERNEST MEISSONIER
Information (General Desaix and the peasant)
On panel, signed and dated *1867*, 12½in by 16in (32cm by 40.5cm)
New York $45,000 (£21,951). 13.X.78

in cultivating the artistic taste of the metropolis'. Two of his most prized paintings were Alfred Stevens's *Ready for the fancy-dress ball* (Fig 1) and Jean Louis Ernest Meissonier's *Information (General Desaix and the peasant)* (Fig 2).

The painting by Stevens, which depicts the Chinese boudoir of his own Paris house, was commissioned from the artist by Vanderbilt on his 1879 trip to Paris. The furnishings of the room were said to have been brought from the Imperial Palace in China. They were very likely loot from the Summer Palace, Peking, which was sacked by Anglo-French military forces in 1860, after which many souvenirs of China found their way to Europe. A contented painter of contemporary elegance, Stevens enjoyed immense popularity in his time. In 1900, he was the first living artist to have a retrospective exhibition of no fewer than 180 paintings at the Ecole des Beaux-Arts.

Even more popular and esteemed was Vanderbilt's favourite artist, Meissonier. The millionaire made a trip to Paris so that Meissonier could paint his portrait and while in the studio bought seven paintings from the artist for the gigantic figure of $188,000. The expenditure of this enormous sum on foreign paintings outraged the American left-wing press which already hated Vanderbilt, who had once unwisely replied to criticisms of service on his railroads with the phrase, 'The public? The public be damned!'. One Socialist writer sneered, 'with the expenditure of a few hundred thousand dollars he instantaneously transformed himself from a heavy-witted uncultured money hoarder into the character of a surpassing judge and patron of art'. For another Meissonier, *The arrival at the château*, he paid $40,000, and for *Information*, which he bought from a Dresden collector, $50,000.

One of Vanderbilt's early biographers wrote that he 'liked pictures which told a story, with either strong or cheerful subjects'. *Information* depicts in careful visual detail an incident from the Napoleonic wars in which General L.C.A. Desaix de Veygoux is interrogating a peasant about the position of two Austrian forces. Vanderbilt was not alone in his admiration for Meissonier. The critical *Gazette des Beaux-Arts* wrote in 1873, 'Meissonier is, perhaps, the most popular artist of our time. If he has a picture at the Salon, the crowd first ascertains where it is, and the obstruction is such that it is not always easy to approach it'. And it was not just the average Salon visitor who was awed by the artist's work. The greatest connoisseurs of the time including Sir Richard Wallace, the Duc d'Aumale (who once bought seventeen works at one time), and Prince Demidoff avidly collected his work. John Ruskin, high priest of taste, admired Meissonier unreservedly and paid a thousand guineas to add the tiny *Napoleon in 1814* to his own collection.

After having been ignored for almost a century these paintings are now returning to favour as indicated by much higher auction prices. *Ready for the fancy-dress ball*, on loan to the Metropolitan Museum of Art between 1885 and 1903, was sold in 1945 for only $1,900, and over forty times as much this season. A feature of New York sales are the purchases made by European dealers and collectors, who sometimes carry off three-quarters of a Salon sale. One hundred years ago American collectors proudly brought these paintings from Paris to the United States. Now the flow is reversing. The paintings are returning to Europe where they are fresh and unknown to the present generation of collectors. At the same time, the reputations of artists like Stevens and Meissonier are shining again, the revived market leading the way to museum exhibitions and critical studies.

The William Henry Vanderbilt art gallery is long gone. The twin Vanderbilt mansions were gradually torn down in the twentieth century, the art gallery was the last section to go, as late as 1947. But the paintings that visitors came to admire on the red velvet walls survive and continue to be redistributed internationally. In 1862, Théophile Gautier, one of the most respected nineteenth-century art critics, wrote of Meissonier, 'he is one of the masters of today who can count on being known in the future'. As Meissonier and his Salon colleagues emerge from their long eclipse it appears that Gautier prophesied correctly.

ANDERS ZORN
Portrait of Antonin Proust
Signed and dated 1888, 41¾in by 54¾in (106cm by 139cm)
London £26,000($53,300). 22.XI.78

EDMOND GEORGES GRANDJEAN
Le boulevard des Italiens, Paris
Signed and dated 1889, 36¾in by 57½in (93.5cm by 146cm)
London £28,000 ($57,400). 22.XI.78
From the collection of the late L. Martineau

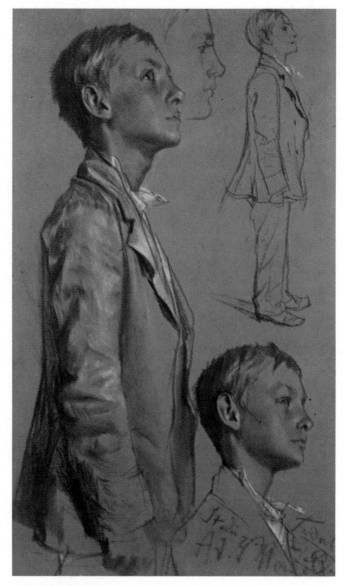

ADOLF VON MENZEL
Friedrich auf Reisen nach Italien
Charcoal heightened with white chalk on buff paper, signed
and inscribed with the title, 15in by $9\frac{1}{2}$in (38cm by 24cm)
London £19,000 ($38,950). 10.V.79

JOAQUIN SOROLLA Y BASTIDA
Swimmers
Signed and dated *1905*, $54\frac{3}{4}$in by $85\frac{1}{2}$in (139cm by 217cm)
New York $135,000 (£65,854). 4.V.79
From the collection of the Metropolitan Museum of Art, New York

FELIX VALLOTTON
Le petit pêcheur à Ivry La Bataille
Signed and dated '24, 28½in by 23¾in (72.5cm by 60.5cm)
Zurich SFr105,000(£29,577:$60,633). 19.V.79

FRANK BUCHSER
Hirtenleben auf dem andalusischen Hochland
Signed with monogram and dated *1859*, 31⅞in by 41⅛in (81cm by 104.5cm)
Zurich SFr55,000(£15,493:$31,761). 19.V.79

JEAN AUGUSTE DOMINIQUE INGRES
Portrait de Monsieur et Madame Edmond Ramel
Pencil heightened with white chalk, signed, inscribed *à mon cher frère Edmond Ramel/Souvenir de Cannes* and dated *1855*, 13½in by 10⅝in (34.3cm by 27cm)
New York $145,000 (£70,732). 7.VI.79
From the collection of the late Benjamin Sonnenberg

THEODORE CHASSERIAU
Portrait de Louis Marcotte de Quivières
Pencil, signed, inscribed *A mon ami Marcotte* and dated *1841*, 13⅛in by 10in (33.5cm by 25.5cm)
New York $102,000 (£49,756). 7.VI.79
From the collection of the late Benjamin Sonnenberg

JEAN-FRANCOIS MILLET
Le vanneur
Signed, *circa* 1847–48, 40½in by 28in (103cm by 71cm)
New York $600,000 (£292,683). 13.X.78

Now in the National Gallery of Art, London

THEODORE CHASSERIAU
Deux jeunes Juives de Constantine berçant un enfant
Signed and dated *1851*, 22½in by 18in (57.2cm by 45.8cm)
Los Angeles $95,000 (£46,341). 12.III.79

JEAN–BAPTISTE–CAMILLE COROT
Vénus au bain
Signed, *circa* 1873, 45¾in by 35¼in (116cm by 89.5cm)
London £240,000 ($492,000). 2.IV.79
From the collection of Mr and Mrs Sydney R. Barlow

This painting is one of the three major classical nude compositions painted by Corot towards the
end of his life, the others being *La toilette* and *Diane au bain*

EDOUARD MANET
Madame Martin en chapeau noir garni de roses
Pastel, signed, 1881, 21¼in by 17¼in (54cm by 44cm)
London £240,000 ($492,000). 2.IV.79
From the collection of Mr and Mrs Sydney R. Barlow

This is one of three portraits, one in oil and two in pastel, which Manet made of Jeanne Martin between 1879 and 1881

PIERRE-AUGUSTE RENOIR
Le pêcheur à la ligne
Signed, 1874, 21¼in by 25¾in (54cm by 65.5cm)
London £610,000 ($1,250,500). 4.VII.79
From the collection of Mr and Mrs Nigel Broackes

CLAUDE MONET
Le pont du chemin de fer à Argenteuil
Signed, 1873, 23in by 38¼in (58.5cm by 97.2cm)
London £420,000 ($861,000). 2.IV.79
From the collection of Mr and Mrs Sydney R. Barlow

This picture was painted in the summer of 1873 on the banks of the Seine at Argenteuil. Monet had an excellent view of this bridge from the house he had rented, which was only some fifty yards from the place where he painted this work

Formerly in the collection of William A. Cargill and sold at Sotheby's on 11 June 1963 for £77,000

GEORGES SEURAT
Le chenal de Gravelines; Petit Fort Philippe
On panel, 1890, 6½in by 9⅞in (16.5cm by 25cm)
London £130,000 ($266,500). 6.XII.78

EUGENE BOUDIN
La plage de Trouville
On panel, signed and dated *Trouville 1863*, 13⅝in by 22⅞in (34.5cm by 58cm)
New York $170,000 (£82,927). 1.XI.78

CAMILLE PISSARRO
Deux jeunes paysannes causant sous les arbres – Pontoise
Signed and dated *'81*, 31¾in by 25½in (80.5cm by 65cm)
London £130,000 ($266,500). 2.IV.79

CLAUDE MONET
Santa Maria della Salute et le Grand Canal, Venise
Signed and dated *1908*, 28¼in by 35¾in (72cm by 91cm)
London £230,000 ($471,500). 2.IV.79

Monet and his wife went to Venice for the first time in 1908. This picture is one of a series that he
painted of this view

GUSTAVE CAILLEBOTTE
Soleils au bord de la Seine
Signed, 1885–86, 36⅜in by 28¾in (92.5cm by 73cm)
New York $70,000 (£34,146). 1.XI.78

PAUL GAUGUIN
Autour des huttes
Signed and dated '87, 34¾in by 21½in (88.4cm by 54.6cm)
New York $350,000 (£170,732). 16.V.79
From the collection of the late Charlotte B. McKim

PAUL CEZANNE
Etude pour 'Les joueurs de cartes'
Circa 1890–92, 19¾in by 18in (50cm by 46cm)
London £370,000 ($758,500). 2.IV.79
From the collection of Mr and Mrs Sydney R. Barlow

This study was painted in Cézanne's studio in the Jas de Bouffant and is one of a series for his two great compositions of card players

Formerly in the collection of Alfred E. Goldschmidt and sold at Sotheby's on 28 October 1970 for $370,000

GEORGES LACOMBE
Les ramasseuses de marrons
1892, 60in by 97¼in (152.4cm by 247cm)
London £37,000 ($75,850). 4.VII.79
From the collection of the Modern Art Foundation, Geneva

MAX PECHSTEIN
Kurische Haüser
Signed and dated *1911*, 20½in by 28⅜in (52cm by 72cm)
New York $50,000 (£24,390). 16.V.79

PABLO PICASSO
Nature morte devant une fenêtre à St Raphaël
Gouache and pencil, signed and dated '19,
13¾in by 9¾in (35cm by 24.8cm)
London £130,000 ($266,500). 3.VII.79
From the collection of the Paul Rosenberg family

PABLO PICASSO
Quatre baigneuses
Tempera on vellum laid on panel, signed and
dated '21, 4in by 6in (10.2cm by 15.3cm)
London £70,000 ($143,500). 3.VII.79
From the collection of the Paul Rosenberg family

Actual size

PABLO PICASSO
Nu assis s'essuyant le pied
Pastel, signed and dated '21, 26in by 20in
(66cm by 50.8cm)
London £280,000 ($574,000). 3.VII.79
From the collection of the Paul Rosenberg family

PABLO PICASSO
La bouteille de vin
Painted in 1925, signed and dated in 1926, 38¾in by 51½in (98.5cm by 130.8cm)
London £460,000 ($943,000). 3.VII.79
From the collection of the Paul Rosenberg family

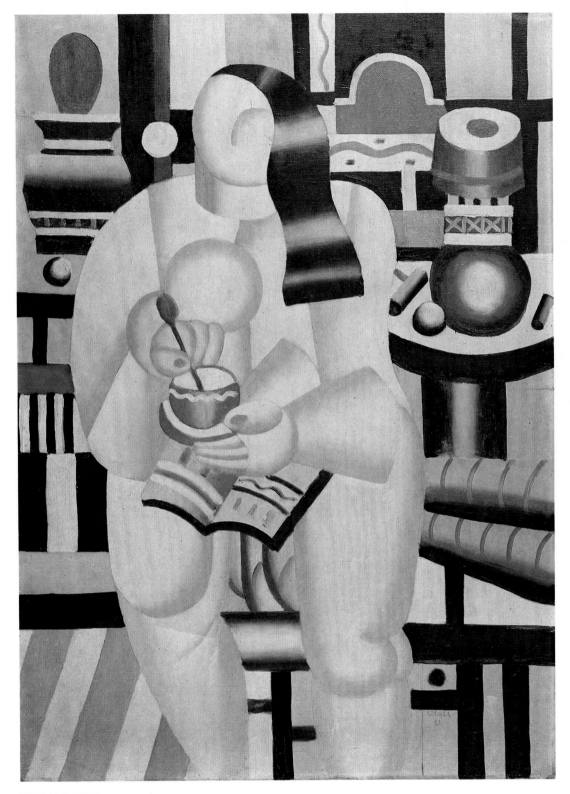

FERNAND LEGER
La tasse de thé
Signed and dated *'21*, 36in by 26½in (91.5cm by 67.3cm)
London £142,000 ($291,100). 3.VII.79
From the collection of the Paul Rosenberg family

PABLO PICASSO
Le sculpteur et sa statue
Pen and ink, watercolour and gouache, signed and dated *Cannes 20 Juillet XXXIII*, 15$\frac{3}{8}$in by 19$\frac{1}{2}$in
(39cm by 49.5cm)
London £152,000 ($311,600). 3.VII.79
From the collection of the Paul Rosenberg family

EGON SCHIELE
Umarmend
Watercolour and tempera with pencil, signed and dated *1913*, 12½in by 19in (32cm by 48.2cm)
New York $120,000 (£58,537). 2.XI.78

GEORGES BRAQUE
La nappe bleue
Oil and sand, signed and dated '38, 34½in by 42in (87.5cm by 106.5cm)
London £190,000($389,500). 3.VII.79
From the collection of the Paul Rosenberg family

WASSILY KANDINSKY
Dorfstrasse, Murnau
On board, signed, 1908, 19in by 27½in (48.3cm by 70cm)
London £165,000($338,250). 2.IV.79
From the collection of Mr and Mrs Sydney Barlow

Formerly in the collection of William H. Weintraub and sold at Sotheby's on 13 May 1970 for $110,000

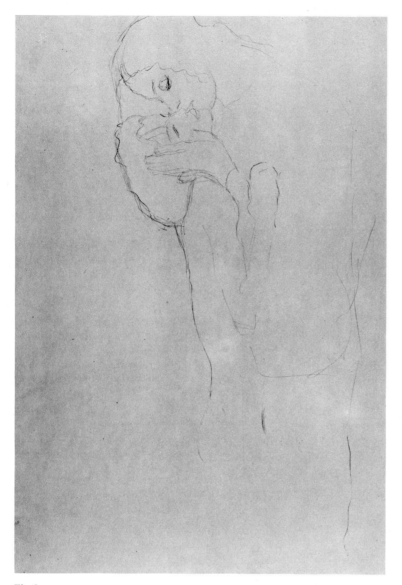

Fig 1
GUSTAV KLIMT
Studie zu 'Wasserschlangen I'
Pencil, atelier stamp, *circa* 1903, 22¼in by 14⅝in (56.5cm by 37cm)
New York $11,000(£5,366). 16.V.79

Fig 2
GUSTAV KLIMT
Wasserschlangen I
Signed, 1904–1907, 19¾in by 7⅞in
(50cm by 20cm)
In the Österreichische Galerie, Vienna

Sketches by Gustav Klimt

Mary-Anne Martin

The thirty-two drawings by Gustav Klimt from the collection of His Highness Prince Sadruddin Aga Khan sold last spring, afford an opportunity to follow the artist's development as a draughtsman from his post-academic style in the 1880s to the erotic shorthand manner of his final years. Although the collection did not contain studies for every major painting, many of the important compositions were represented, and it is possible from these drawings to gain some insight into Klimt's artistic process.

As early as 1922, Gustav Glueck, then director of the Gemäldegalerie des Kunsthistorischen Museums in Vienna, observed that 'Gustav Klimt belongs without a doubt among the greatest draughtsmen of his time, and his drawings alone are certain to assure him a place in the history of art'.[1] More than fifty years later it is apparent that Klimt's drawings are much closer in temperament to our own epoch than the paintings to which they relate. While such elaborate symbolist works as *Der Kuss* and the first *Bildnis von Adele Bloch-Bauer* (Fig 4) are securely bound to the period of Art Nouveau and the Vienna of Sigmund Freud and Richard Strauss, the related drawings appear both immediate and timeless to the contemporary viewer.

Klimt observed and sketched his sitters in every possible aspect, recording spontaneous gestures and moods. He encouraged his nude models to wander freely in his studio, pausing to chat or to assume poses at will; these attitudes he would render in swift strokes for later use in his formal compositions. One such study for *Wasserschlangen I* (Fig 1) evokes an embrace with a few delicate lines which briefly emphasise the faces meeting in a tender kiss, then gradually vanish on the page. Klimt was able to attain this masterful economy of line only by systematically rejecting the highlighting, shading, perspective and anatomical realism so laboriously insisted upon in his student years at the Kunstgewerbeschule des Österreichischen Museums für Kunst und Industrie.

In the painted version of *Wasserschlangen I* (Fig 2) the spontaneous kiss of the sketch has been lost, as the 'women friends' float together in an aquatic reverie, their hair a mass of undulating golden threads, entwined with spiralling sea creatures. Now the composition has been removed from the area of recognisable human experience into a realm of mystic significance.

No less remarkable is the final *Bildnis von Adele Bloch-Bauer I* when considered in relation to the numerous studies Klimt made for this painting (Figs 3 and 5). Prince Sadruddin's collection alone contained eight such sketches and there were reputedly hundreds. Adele is seen in an armchair, leaning to the left, sitting straight, turned one

Fig 4
GUSTAV KLIMT
Bildnis von Adele Bloch-Bauer I
Signed and dated *1907*, 54¼in by 54¼in
(138cm by 138cm)
In the Österreichische Galerie, Vienna

Fig 3
GUSTAV KLIMT
Studie zu 'Bildnis von Adele Bloch-Bauer I'
Charcoal on buff paper, *circa* 1902,
17½in by 12½in (44.5cm by 31.5cm)
New York $10,000 (£4,878). 16.V.79

way and another, sometimes smiling, sometimes bored, even completely faceless. There are also standing versions and sketches of her shoes and dresses.

In the finished portrait of 1907, considered the finest example of Klimt's 'golden' period, Adele is rendered as a hieratic figure, almost stifled by the golden layers of ornament which compose her environment. It is noted that Klimt made a trip to Italy in 1903, where he was much taken with the mosaics of San Vitale. Certainly a comparison of the finished portrait of Adele Bloch-Bauer with the mosaic portrait of Theodora strongly bespeaks this influence. Could it be that Klimt suggests a parallel between the situation of this wealthy wife of a Viennese businessman and the Byzantine empress of the sixth century AD?

The boldly sexual *Studie für 'Die Braut'* (Fig 6) brings out a particularly interesting aspect of the relationship between Klimt's drawings and paintings, one that might have passed unnoticed had it not been that this painting (Fig 7) was found in an incomplete stage in the artist's studio at the time of his death in 1918. The pose in the drawing is typical of Klimt, who was too straightforward in his artistic approach to employ the customary device of a modestly placed hand or a bit of drapery. In the painting Klimt was in the process of covering the explicitly rendered pubic area of the bride with a decorative overlay of suggestive and symbolic ornamental shapes. It is quite likely that had he lived to complete the work, this evidence of the – in this case, literally – underlying sexual basis of Klimt's decorative ornament would have been

Fig 5
GUSTAV KLIMT
Studie zu 'Bildnis von Adele Bloch-Bauer I'
Charcoal and red crayon on buff paper, *circa* 1902, $17\frac{3}{4}$in by $12\frac{3}{4}$in
(45cm by 32.5cm)
New York $5,500 (£2,683). 16.V.79

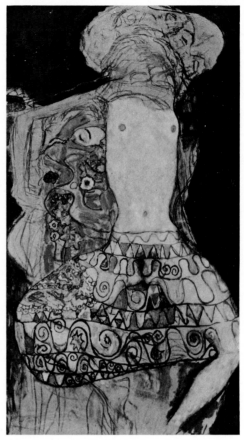

Fig 6
GUSTAV KLIMT
Studie für 'Die Braut'
Pencil, atelier stamp, *circa* 1916, 22¼in by 14¾in
(56.5cm by 37.5cm)
New York $13,000(£6,341). 16.V.79

Fig 7
GUSTAV KLIMT
Die Braut (detail)
1917–18, 55½in by 75in (141cm by 190cm)
Private collection, on loan to the
Österreichische Galerie, Vienna

hidden, left to the speculation of future art historians. Instead, Klimt has provided
them with a valuable clue to his creative methods. While Freud was probing the
unconscious mind, stripping away layers of myth and symbol to reveal the sexual
nature of man, Klimt, keenly aware of his sexual self, was cloaking his creations in
veils of symbolic and erotic ornament.

The key position of the drawings in this process emerges quite clearly. These
fragmentary observations, caught in the studio, pages drawn from life and frequently
left in piles around his working area, are the pulse beats of his oeuvre, 'mere indication
and abbreviation . . . perhaps the ultimate of Klimt's artistic achievement'.[2]

[1]   Gustav Glueck, *Gustav Klimt: Zehn Handzeichnungen*, Vienna, 1922 (reprinted in translation in the
catalogue for the exhibition, *Gustav Klimt*, Galerie St Etienne, New York, 1970), p 10
[2]   Ibid
The author would like to acknowledge her debt to the following: Alfred Werner, *Gustav Klimt, One
hundred drawings*, New York, 1972; and Alessandra Comini, *Gustav Klimt*, New York, 1975

PABLO PICASSO
Trois danseurs au repos
Pen and ink on blue-grey paper, signed and
dated '25, 13¾in by 9⅞in (35cm by 25cm)
London £56,000($114,800). 3.VII.79
From the collection of the Paul Rosenberg family

EDVARD MUNCH
Abend – Melancholie
Charcoal, varnished, signed, 1892,
6½in by 13in (16.5cm by 33cm)
London £23,000($47,150). 4.IV.79

This drawing was used for the illustration or
'vignette' as the frontispiece of Emanuel
Goldstein's collection of poems, *Alruner*,
published in Oslo in the autumn of 1892

PAUL KLEE
Adam und Evchen
Pen and ink and watercolour, signed, inscribed with the title and dated *1921*,
12⅜in by 8¾in (31.4cm by 22cm)
New York $100,000(£48,780). 2.XI.78

EMIL NOLDE
Zwei Mädchen
Watercolour and gouache on japan paper, signed, *circa* 1925, 23in by 18in
(58.5cm by 45.7cm)
New York $75,000(£36,585). 16.V.79

PAVEL TCHELITCHEW
Portrait of Serge Lifar
Pen and brown ink and wash, signed and dated *Paris 1931*,
10in by 8¼in (25.3cm by 21cm)
London £2,700 ($5,535). 6.VI.79

ALEXANDRE BENOIS
Léon Bakst at Martychkino station
Pencil, signed and dated *1896*, 11½in by 6⅞in
(29cm by 17.5cm)
London £5,000 ($10,250). 6.VI.79

LEON BAKST
Design for the decor of 'Jeux'
Pencil on paper laid down on
canvas, signed, *circa* 1914,
29in by 41in (73.5cm by 104cm)
London £3,700 ($7,585). 6.VI.79

NATALIA GONTCHAROVA
Design for the decor of Act 1 of 'Coq d'or'
Watercolour and pencil, signed and dated *Paris 1914*, 13in by $17\frac{7}{8}$in (33cm by 45.5cm)
New York $10,500 (£5,122). 24.XI.78
From the collection of William W. Appleton

PAVEL FILONOV
The Flight into Egypt
1918, 28in by 35in (71cm by 89cm)
New York $33,000(£16,098). 3.XI.78

EL LISSITZKY
Proun 4 B
Gouache, watercolour and pencil on buff paper, inscribed *P4B*, *circa* 1920,
$8\frac{5}{8}$in by $6\frac{7}{8}$in (22cm by 17.5cm)
New York $26,000 (£12,683). 3.XI.78

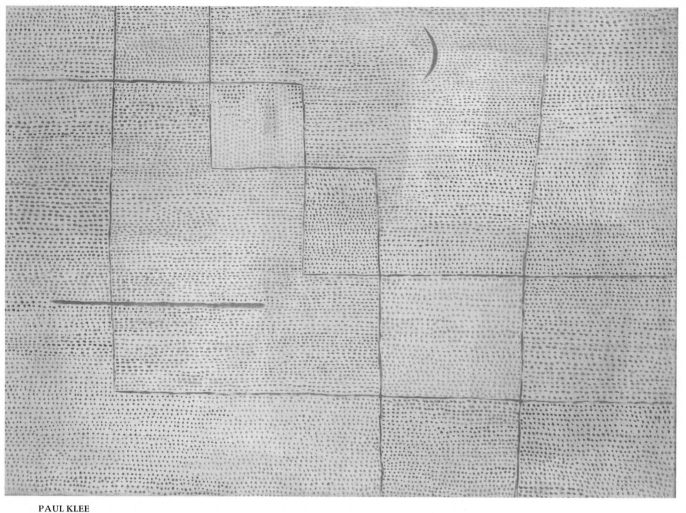

PAUL KLEE
Die Klaerung
Signed, 1932, 27½in by 37⅞in (69.8cm by 96.2cm)
New York $435,000 (£212,195). 17.V.79

ALBERTO GIACOMETTI
Bust of Diego
Bronze, signed and dated *1953*, height 13¼in (33.6cm)
New York $77,000 (£37,561). 9.VI.79
From the collection of the late Benjamin Sonnenberg

SALVADOR DALI
Le pharmacien d'Ampurdan ne cherchant absolument rien
On panel, signed and dated *1936*, 11¾in by 20½in (30cm by 52cm)
London £85,000 ($174,250). 6.XII.78
From the collection of Edward F.W. James; now in the Museum Folkwang, Essen

RENE MAGRITTE
La grande guerre
Signed and inscribed with the title on the reverse, 1964, 25½in by 21¼in (65cm by 54cm)
London £112,000 ($229,600). 2.IV.79

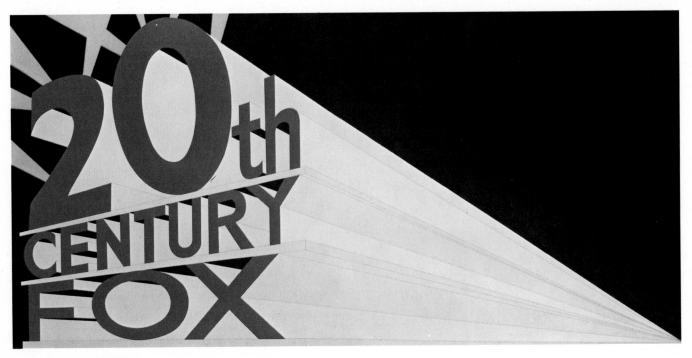

EDWARD RUSCHA
Large trademark with eight spotlights (20th Century Fox with searchlights)
1962, 132in by 67in (335.5cm by 170cm)
New York $57,500 (£28,049). 2.XI.78

MORRIS LOUIS
Gamma Rho
Acrylic, 1960, $102\frac{1}{2}$in by $164\frac{1}{4}$in (260.5cm by 417cm)
New York $115,000 (£56,098). 2.XI.78

KENNETH NOLAND
Paint
Acrylic, dated *1959* on the reverse, 72½in by 69¾in (184cm by 177cm)
London £20,000 ($41,000). 5.XII.78

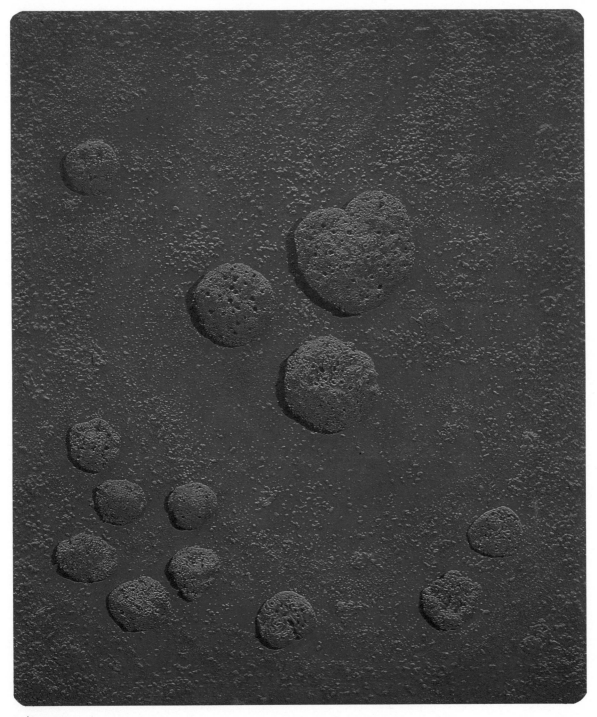

YVES KLEIN
Relief d'éponges – RE 11 bleu
Sponges, pebbles and blue pigment on panel, 1960, 78¾in by 65in (200cm by 165cm)
London £43,000 ($88,150). 5.IV.79

LOUISE NEVELSON
Unit of seven
Gold-painted wood on wood base, signed and dated *1960*, 78in by 62in (198cm by 157.5cm)
New York $25,000 (£12,195). 17.V.79

ASGER JORN
Ballet immobile
Signed, inscribed with the title and dated '57 on the reverse, 63¾in by 51¼in (162cm by 130cm)
London £13,500 ($27,675). 5.XII.78

WILLIAM MICHAEL HARNETT
Still life with violin
On panel, signed and dated *Paris 1885*, 21½in by 17¾in (54.5cm by 45cm)
New York $300,000 (£146,341). 20.IV.79

EASTMAN JOHNSON, after EMANUEL LEUTZE
Washington crossing the Delaware
Inscribed *E. Leutze*, 1851, 40½in by 68in (103cm by 173cm)
New York $370,000 (£180,488). 20.IV.79

In 1850 the German-born American history painter, Emanuel Leutze, produced his gigantic masterpiece, *Washington crossing the Delaware*, now in the Metropolitan Museum of Art, New York. It was an immediate success in Europe and Mr Goupil, of Goupil, Vibert & Co, New York, went to Leutze's studio in Dusseldorf to negotiate the purchase of a second painting as well as a small, more portable version, suitable for engraving. As Leutze had already completed one large and one small work and was in the process of producing a second large canvas, he asked Eastman Johnson, who had recently attached himself to Leutze's studio to study history painting, to do the smaller, printer's version. This is documented in a letter written by Johnson to a friend, dated March 1851, 'Since the first of January I have been with Leutze. Our studio is a large hall where six of us paint with convenience. Three on large pictures. The chief is Leutze's Washington crossing the Delaware . . . It is already perhaps two-thirds finished and I am making a copy on a reduced scale from which an engraving is to be made. It is sold to the International [A]rt Union of New York and will be exhibited throughout the States in the Fall.' Although the present painting is inscribed with Leutze's name it has been pointed out that the area around it has been smeared and that perhaps another inscription had been rubbed out and Leutze's signature added

THOMAS POLLACK ANSHUTZ
The farmer and his son at harvesting
Signed and dated *1879*, 24¼in by 17¼in (61.5cm by 43.8cm)
New York $110,000(£53,659). 20.IV.79

FREDERIC EDWIN CHURCH
New England landscape
Signed, *circa* 1849–52, 25in by 36in (63.5cm by 91.4cm)
New York $230,000 (£112,195). 27.X.78

WINSLOW HOMER
Two boys rowing
Watercolour, signed, *circa* 1880, 10in by 13¾in (25.4cm by 35cm)
New York $150,000 (£73,171). 20.IV.79

FREDERICK CHILDE HASSAM
Yachts, Gloucester Harbor
Signed, 1899, 34in by 36½in (86.4cm by 92.7cm)
Los Angeles $90,000 (£43,902). 18.VI.79
From the collection of the San Francisco Art Institute

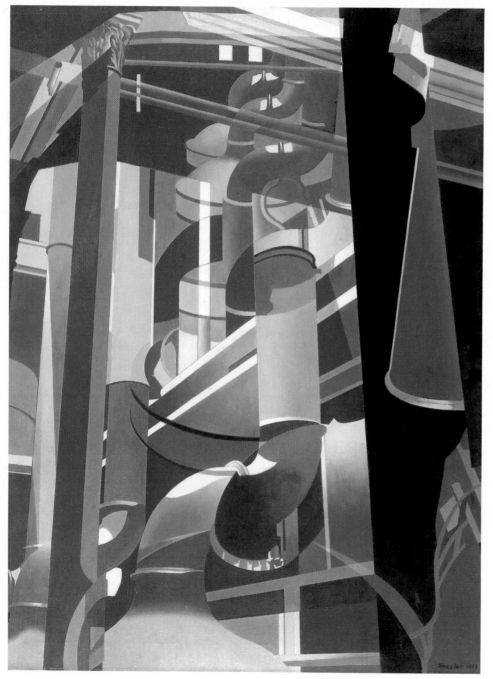

CHARLES SHEELER
Convolusions
Signed and dated *1952*, 36in by 26in (91.5cm by 66cm)
New York $120,000 (£58,537). 20.IV.79
From the collection of the Illinois Institute of Technology, Chicago

THOMAS HART BENTON
Instruction
Tempera, signed, *circa* 1940, 33in by 40in (83.8cm by 101.5cm)
New York $105,000 (£51,220). 27.X.78

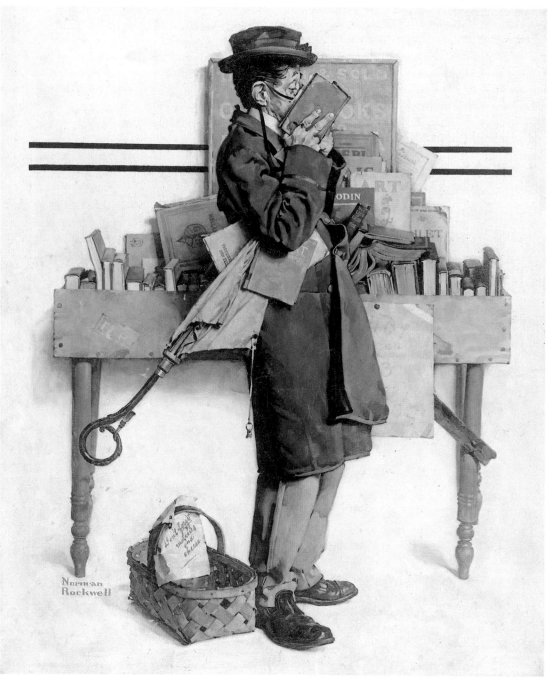

NORMAN ROCKWELL
The bookworm
Signed, 32in by 26in (81.3cm by 66cm)
New York $65,000(£31,707). 20.IV.79

This work appeared as the cover illustration of *The Saturday Evening Post* on 14 August 1926

GEORGIA O'KEEFFE
Red poppy
Painted in 1927, signed, inscribed with the title and dated *1928* on the reverse,
7in by 9in (17.8cm by 22.9cm)
New York $82,500 (£40,244). 20.IV.79
From the collection of the late Daniel Catton Rich

CHARLES MARION RUSSELL
After his first hunt
Pencil and watercolour heightened with bodycolour, signed, $18\frac{1}{4}$in by $22\frac{1}{4}$in (46.3cm by 56.5cm)
London £30,000 ($61,500). 27.IX.78
From the collection of Mrs N. Livesley

Opposite above
CLARENCE ALPHONSE GAGNON, RCA
Crépuscule, les Laurentides
Signed and inscribed with the title, $19\frac{3}{4}$in by $25\frac{1}{2}$in (50.2cm by 64.8cm)
Toronto Can $40,000 (£16,667:$34,167). 14.V.79

Opposite below
CORNELIUS KRIEGHOFF
Making maple syrup
Signed, inscribed with the title and dated *1853*, 12in by 18in (30.5cm by 45.7cm)
Toronto Can $50,000 (£20,833:$42,708). 14.V.79

HECTOR HYPPOLITE
St John surrounded by flowers
On masonite, signed and inscribed with the title, before 1948, 30in by 24in (76.2cm by 61cm)
PB Eighty-four $11,000(£5,366). 23.V.79
From the collection of Julia Marshall

JOSÉ MARIA VELASCO
Valle de Mexico
Signed and dated *Mexico 1892*, 22½in by 30½in (57cm by 77.5cm)
New York $115,000 (£56,098). 11.V.79
From the collection of Mrs Henry Ehlers

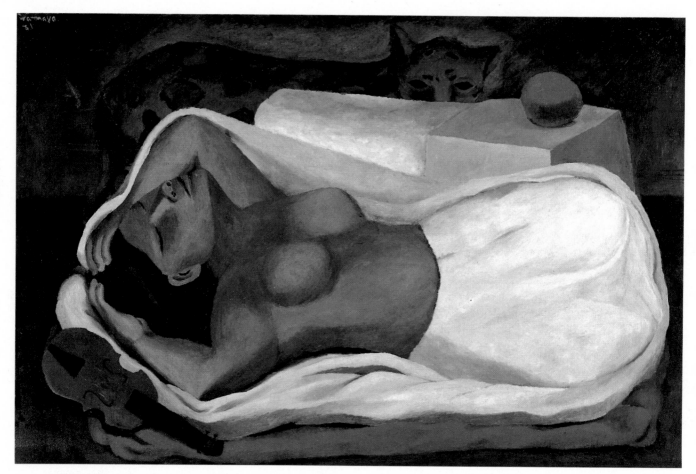

RUFINO TAMAYO
Mujer dormida
On linen, signed and dated *'31*, 33¾in by 49⅜in (85.7cm by 125.5cm)
New York $77,500 (£37,805). 11.V.79
From the collection of Russell Padget

Prints

PABLO PICASSO
Buste de femme d'après Cranach le Jeune
Linoleum cut, signed, 1958, 25$\frac{3}{8}$in by 21$\frac{1}{8}$in (64.5cm by 53.5cm)
New York $85,000 (£41,463). 16.II.79

SOUTH GERMAN SCHOOL
St Augustine and the Child
Engraving, *circa* 1450–65, 7⅝in by 4⅞in (19.2cm by 12.5cm)
London £23,000 ($47,150). 26.IV.79

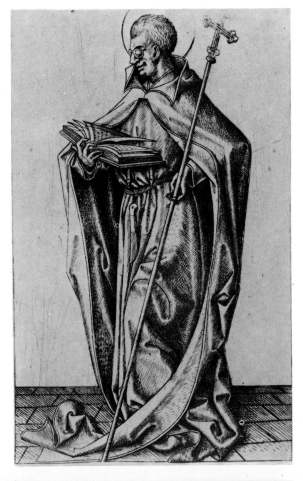

THE MASTER E.S.
St Philip
Engraving, *circa* 1450–60, 5¾in by 3½in (14.6cm by 9cm)
London £12,000 ($24,600). 26.IV.79

ISRAHEL VAN MECKENEM
Children playing
Engraving, after 1497, the second
state of three, 4½in by 5⅝in
(11.5cm by 14.3cm)
London £9,000 ($18,450). 1.XI.78

REMBRANDT HARMENSZ. VAN RIJN
Clement de Jonghe, printseller
Etching with drypoint, the fourth state of six, $8\frac{1}{4}$in by $6\frac{3}{8}$in (20.9cm by 16.2cm)
New York $37,500 (£18,293). 16.II.79
From the collection of Mr and Mrs W. Clifford Klenk

SIR ANTHONY VAN DYCK
Jan Brueghel the Elder
Etching, the first state of seven, $9\frac{5}{8}$in by $6\frac{1}{8}$in (24.4cm by 15.7cm)
New York $46,000(£22,439). 16.II.79
From the collection of Mr and Mrs W. Clifford Klenk

PRINCE RUPERT OF THE RHINE
The standard bearer
Mezzotint, the second state of three, $10\frac{7}{8}$in by $7\frac{1}{2}$in (27.7cm by 19cm)
London £12,000 ($24,600). 1.XI.78

Que biene el Coco.

FRANCISCO JOSÉ DE GOYA Y LUCIENTES
Los caprichos
Etching and aquatint, a set of eighty trial proofs before the first edition of 1799 and before the correction of titles on five of the plates, each approximately $8\frac{1}{2}$in by $5\frac{7}{8}$in (21.5cm by 15cm), contemporary Spanish binding
London £82,500 ($169,125). 26.IV.79

After JOHN JAMES AUDUBON
Great American cock male (wild turkey)
Hand-coloured engraving and aquatint, 1829,
39⅜in by 26⅜in (100cm by 67cm)
New York $13,500 (£6,585). 1.II.79

THE NORTH PARADE.

JOHN ROBERT COZENS
Views of Bath
One of a set of eight etchings
with grey wash, published
30 November 1773, each
approximately 11in by 15in
(28cm by 38cm)
Belgravia £6,500 ($13,325).
25.V.79

MESSIDOR

After LOUIS LAFITTE
Les mois républicains
One of a set of twelve stipple engravings finished by hand, each approximately
$13\frac{3}{4}$in by $10\frac{5}{8}$in (34.9cm by 26.9cm)
Belgravia £2,800 ($5,740). 29.IX.78

EDVARD MUNCH
Mädchen auf der Brücke
Lithograph and woodcut on wove, signed, 1920, 19$\frac{7}{8}$in by 17$\frac{1}{8}$in (50.5cm by 43.5cm)
London £46,000 ($94,300). 17.V.79

EDVARD MUNCH
Vampyr
Lithograph and woodcut on
chine, a proof impression,
signed, *circa* 1895,
15⅛in by 21⅞in
(38.5cm by 55.5cm)
London £30,000 ($61,500).
14.XII.78

EDVARD MUNCH
Der Kuss
Woodcut on japan paper,
signed and inscribed
(Lashilly), 1902,
18⅜in by 18⅜in
(46.6cm by 46.6cm)
London £25,000 ($51,250).
14.XII.78

OTTO MUELLER
Ein in Dünen sitzendes, und ein liegendes Mädchen
Lithograph on wove, signed, 1920, 11½in by 15⅜in (29.3cm by 39cm)
London £5,000 ($10,250). 17.V.79

MARC CHAGALL
Daphnis and Chloe: death of Dorcon
Lithograph, signed, 1961, 16¾in by 25¼in (42.5cm by 64.1cm)
Florida $15,000 (£7,317). 20.III.79

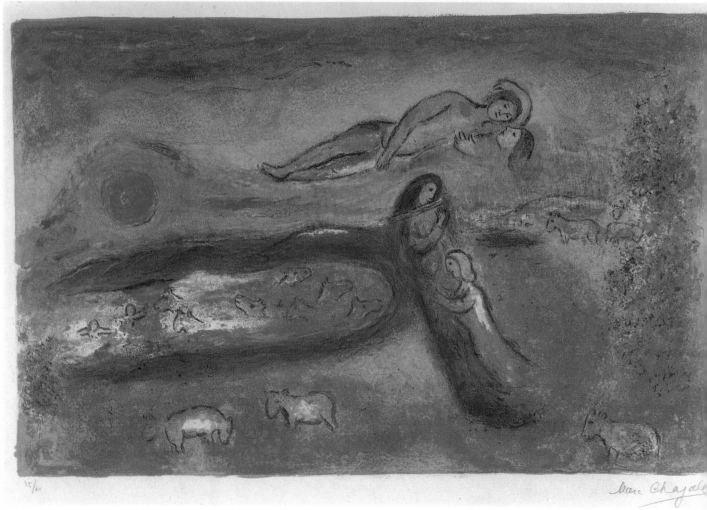

HENRI MATISSE
Marie-José – la robe jaune
Aquatint, signed, *circa* 1950, 21$\frac{1}{8}$in by 16$\frac{1}{2}$in (53.8cm by 41.9cm)
London £9,200 ($18,860). 14.XII.78
From the collection of Madame Roger Lacourière

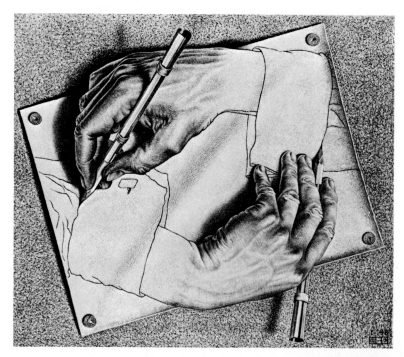

MAURITS CORNELIS ESCHER
Drawing hands
Lithograph, signed,
1948, 11⅛in by 13⅛in
(28.2cm by 33.3cm)
Los Angeles $11,000 (£5,366).
5.II.79

MAX KLINGER
Brahmsphantasie: Fest (Reigen)
Etching and drypoint, signed and dated *8 Nov. 93*, 10in by 13¾in (25.3cm by 35cm)
New York $3,800 (£1,854). 9.V.79

Manuscripts and
Printed Books

GHIYAS UD-DIN IBN HUMAN UD-DIN called KHWAND AMIR
Habib Us-Siyar, a Persian manuscript illustrated with five Turkish
seventeenth-century miniature paintings, Tabriz, 1525–50
New York $44,000 (£21,463). 15.XII.78.

This miniature shows Prince Tahmasp making obeisance before his
father, Shah Isma'il

Farhad visits Shirin, a Timurid miniature, Herat, mid fifteenth century
London £30,000 ($61,500). 24.IV.79

The Qur'an, two vellum leaves in *ma'il* (slanting) script, Medina, eighth century
London £42,000 ($86,100). 23.IV.79
From the collection of the Hagop Kevorkian Fund

The *ma'il* script was a precursor of *kufik* and *naskh* calligraphy, and the few known
examples are the earliest surviving Qur'anic texts

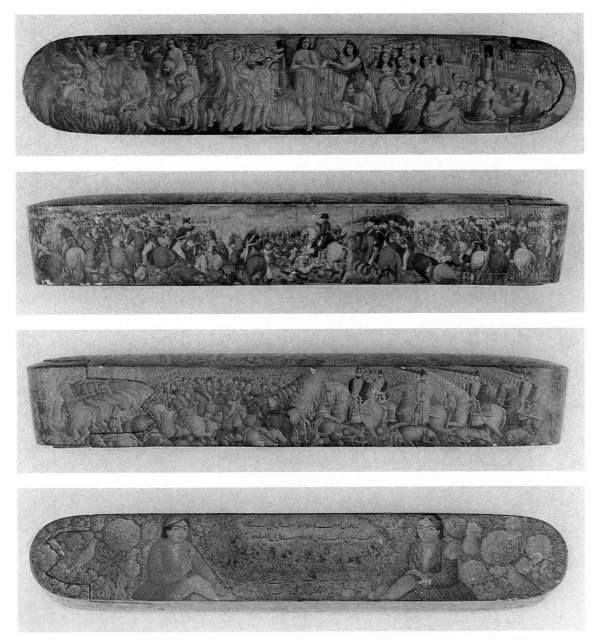

Four views of a Persian Qajar lacquer pen-box painted by the Painter Laureate, 1847, completed by Isma'il Jala'ir, signed and dated *17 May 1853*, Tabriz, length 9¾in (24.7cm)
London £45,000 ($92,250). 9.X.78

The scenes represented on this pen-box are the Last Judgement, Napoleon leading his troops in battle, Nasr ad-Din Shah leading his troops against the Afghans before Herat, and two young men with an inscription by Jala'ir. The first two are by the Painter Laureate. In a contemporary account (*Voyage en Turquie et en Perse exécuté par ordre du gouvernement français*, Paris, 1854) Xavier Hommaire de Hell relates, 'Today we were visited by the most celebrated painter of Persia, who has been deaf and dumb for about forty years. As an example of his work he brought us a pen-box covered with paintings; the subject was Hell and Paradise. . . . This pen-box is unfinished, and will eventually bear on one of its sides a drawing of a scene from the life of Napoleon I, after a French picture'

The foundation charter of Westminster Abbey with the Great Seal of Edward the Confessor, a manuscript on vellum, dated *5 Kal. Jan. 1066* (28 December 1065), written in the early twelfth century
London £58,000 ($118,900). 19.VI.79
From the collection of the Rt Hon Earl of Winchilsea and Nottingham

Edward the Confessor, who founded Westminster Abbey, died a week after its consecration without having issued a charter. This one was written in his name by the monks of the Abbey within eighty years of his death and throughout the Middle Ages was regarded as the original

HORACE
Carminum Liber, an illuminated
manuscript, north-east Italy (probably
Venice), *circa* 1460–80
London £16,000 ($32,800). 19.VI.79
From the collection of His Grace the
Duke of Wellington

This is one of ten medieval manuscripts
stolen from the Spanish Royal Library by
Joseph Bonaparte and captured from his
coach at the Battle of Vitoria on 21 June
1813. The French were defeated by an
allied army led by the Duke of Wellington
who was given charge of the contents of
the coach. He offered to return the
manuscripts to the King of Spain but on
29 November 1816, Ferdinand VII asked
the Duke to accept them as a gift

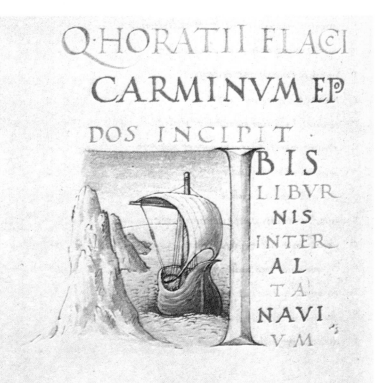

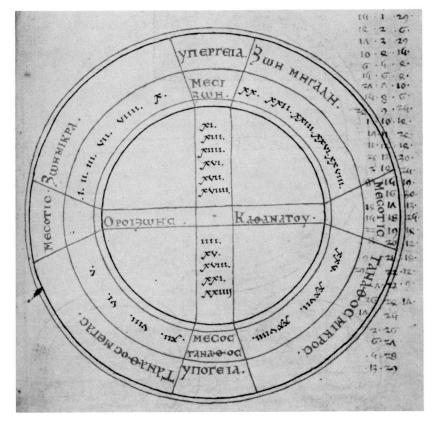

An anthology of Romanesque science
comprising many texts on science,
medicine, astronomy, architecture,
music and geography, a manuscript
on vellum, early twelfth century
London £22,000 ($45,100). 2.V.79
From the Honeyman Collection

AD·ALFONSVM·CLARISSIMVM
ARAGONVM·REGEM·IANNO
ZII·MANETTI·DE·TERREMOTV·LI
BER·PRIMVS·INCIPIT·PREFATIO

VO·QVIDAM·NO
ui et inusitati Sere
nissime princeps ce
terorum omnium co
tinuorum ac per spa
tium dierum circiter
sexaginta quotidiano
rum terremotus tuis felicibus fortunatis
q; temporibus quadringentesimo quinqua
gesimo sexto supra millesimum christiane
salutis anno in medio hiemis altero inge
tiori secundo nonas decembris noctu : al
tero uero interdiu secundo Kalendas ia
nuarii : cum magna plurium pagorum
ac opidorum urbiumq; euersione atq;
seua et truculenta multarum gentium
strage non modo per uniuersam campa
niam ueterem : sed per totam quoq; luca

Campania
uetus.

Book of Hours, the Arrest of Christ, one miniature from an illuminated manuscript on vellum, Germany, possibly Nuremberg, early sixteenth century
London £16,000 ($32,800). 5.XII.78

Opposite
GIANNOZZO MANETTI
De Terremotu, an illuminated manuscript on vellum, Naples, *circa* 1457–60
London £11,000 ($22,550). 2.V.79
From the Honeyman Collection

This treatise on the movements of the earth was inspired by the earthquakes in Naples on 4 and 31 December 1456 witnessed by the author. It is dedicated to Alfonso of Aragon, King of Naples

Machzor Rome, a Hebrew manuscript on vellum written by the scribe Meir ben Shmuel Deslois for Yechiel ben Matatyah, containing the Liturgy for the whole year according to the Roman rite, Pisa, 1397
Zurich SFr210,000 (£59,155:$121,268). 21.XI.78
From the collection of the late David Solomon Sassoon

Sefirat Ha'Omer, a Hebrew manuscript on vellum, possibly Amsterdam, 1705, the engraved gold covers, Germany or Austria, early eighteenth century
London £5,500 ($11,275). 29.I.79

This is the smallest Hebrew booklet known and measures only $\frac{3}{4}$in by $\frac{5}{8}$in (1.7cm by 1.5cm)

The de Castro Pentateuch, a manuscript Bible in Hebrew on vellum with fourteen illuminated pages, written by the scribe Levi ben David Ha'Levi for Joseph ben Ephraim, possibly Germany, 1344
Zurich SFr700,000 (£197,183:$404,225). 21.XI.78
From the collection of the late David Solomon Sassoon

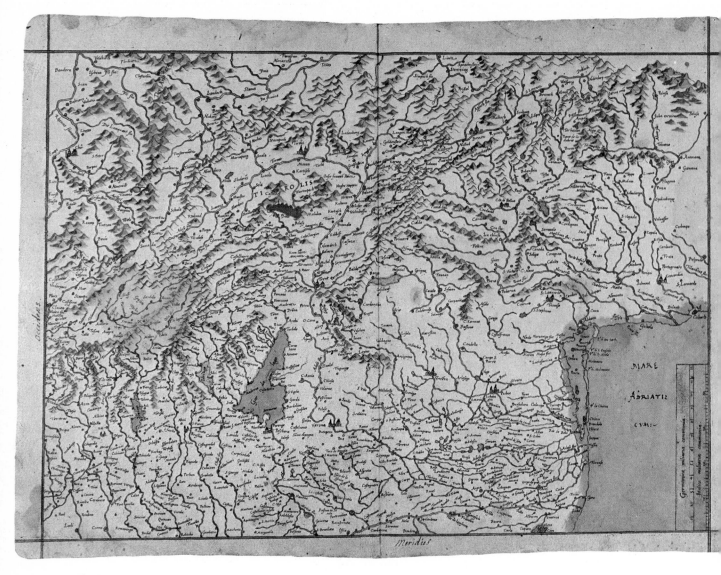

Fig 1
GERARD MERCATOR
Tirolis & pars Lombardiae
A manuscript map, *circa* 1570

The Mercator Atlas was sold as one lot in London on 13 March 1979 for £340,000 ($697,000)

The Mercator Atlas of Europe

A. S. Osley

It was in October 1966 in Haarlem that I light-heartedly promised to translate a little Latin treatise on italic lettering by Gerard Mercator (1512–94). Having completed the work, I began to ask myself how Mercator had learned the italic script, why he had done so and whether his book had had any influence on the handwriting of his contemporaries. Almost without thinking I had launched myself on a far-reaching inquiry with some unexpected consequences.

The more one studied Mercator, the more one came to admire him. A man of naturally sweet disposition, he was born in the Netherlands of humble parents and attained great eminence entirely by his own efforts. Most people are aware of his reputation as a cartographer, but this is only one facet of his genius. He was an extraordinarily skilled engraver both in wood and copper. He constructed exquisite scientific instruments and globes. He was an erudite student of the Scriptures and a keen student of antiquity. Annotations in his hand can be seen on some pages of the fifth-century Codex Argenteus (the earliest specimen of written Teutonic language), now in Uppsala but for some years in the possession of the Mercator family. His cartographic studies yielded two fundamental innovations for the assistance of mariners: the representation of the world on the projection named after him, and proof that the magnetic pole which caused deviations in the compass needle was terrestrial not celestial. Throughout his life he maintained a learned correspondence with scholars all over the world. My primary interest, however, was in Mercator's lettering. By the end of 1968 I was able to demonstrate that here too he was an innovator and that he had radically changed the face of maps in the sixteenth-century Netherlands.

It so happened that, only a few weeks before I began my translation, a Dutch schoolteacher, Tom Varekamp, was on holiday in Belgium. He went to Brussels looking for old prints of Amsterdam, of which he was a collector. Under a pile of dusty magazines in a bookshop he noticed two well-worn folio atlases, which had lain there for over six years. The interesting thing was that the atlases were not of a regular kind but had been especially put together for some individual purpose. Varekamp, although he lacked a technical knowledge of cartography, could see that some of the

Fig 2
GERARD MERCATOR
Europae Universalis

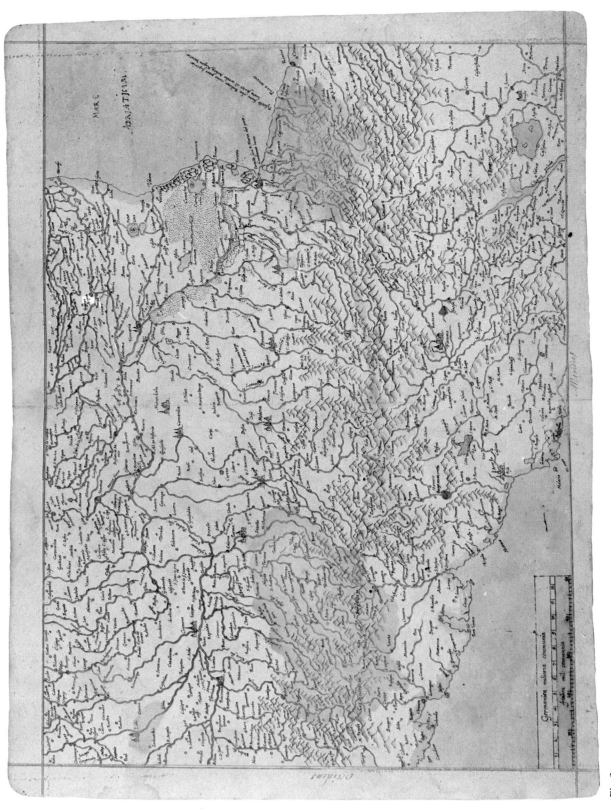

Fig 3
GERARD MERCATOR
Lombardiae reliquii
A manuscript map, *circa* 1570

maps were by good names such as Blaeu, Mercator, Jansson and Hondius. He decided to buy the atlases. A few weeks later, he consulted a dealer as to their value for insurance purposes. The dealer confirmed that some of the maps were rare and that others might have been cut up from large printed wall-maps. He was less intrigued by the two manuscript maps in one of the atlases and thought them to have been made by 'a good amateur'.

Varekamp spent several months studying the contents of that atlas and in the process acquired a detailed familiarity with the work of sixteenth-century cartographers in the Netherlands. He established that maps in the atlas had indeed been cut from rare wall-maps of Europe and of the British Isles made by Gerard Mercator. After a year he had further satisfied himself that the manuscript maps were also the work of Mercator because of their resemblance to printed maps. The question then was whether the manuscripts were from Mercator's own hand. This was important because no other examples were known.

At this point the independent paths of Varekamp and myself converged. In the summer of 1968, the late R. A. Skelton, Superintendent of the Map Room at the British Museum, sent me copies of the manuscripts. Then in September of that year, while visiting Amsterdam, I was introduced to the owner who showed me the atlas in his home. Being at that time completely saturated in Mercator's style of lettering as a result of the quite separate researches mentioned above, I could see immediately that the handwritten titles which occurred throughout the atlas were without doubt by Gerard Mercator. Further examination convinced me that the manuscript maps, which were in a smaller script suitable for engraving, had also been lettered by him.

To be more precise, the atlas contained the only extant examples of Mercator's wall-map of Europe, 1554 (the one at Breslau was destroyed in 1945 during the war), nine maps having been obtained by cutting up at least four wall-maps (Fig 4); the fourth known copy of Mercator's wall-map of the British Isles, 1564 (six atlas maps from at least three wall-maps); parts of Mercator's wall-map of the world, 1569, of which only three other copies are recorded (Fig 2); thirty maps from Abraham Ortelius's published atlas of 1570; an Italian map of Ancona; and the unique double-folio manuscript maps by Mercator, *Tirolis & pars Lombardiae* (Fig 1) and *Lombardiae reliquii* (Fig 3).

The atlas was almost certainly compiled to serve as a working guide for a traveller in Europe who was particularly interested in Italy. The lavish cutting-up of expensive wall-maps (another indication that the atlas originated in Mercator's workshop) postulates an important patron. Evidence suggests that this was probably Werner von Gymnich. In 1570 he was appointed guardian of the Crown Prince Karl Friedrich of Cleves, whom he accompanied on travels through Europe from 1572 until the Crown Prince died in Rome in 1575. The atlas eventually found its way to the Cistercian monastery of Mariawald, where Alanus Ortmans repaired, re-arranged and rebound it in 1771, adding notes and an index. The library of the monastery of Mariawald was dispersed in 1797–98 by the French Revolutionary Government.

Thus it became clear that the atlas by Mercator was a unique treasure, not only for the precious individual items which it contained, but in its totality as an artifact from the hands of the master himself.

Fig 4
GERARD MERCATOR
Britannicae Insulae
Part of the printed wall-map of Europe, 1554

VASLAV FOMICH NIJINSKY
The autograph manuscript of his diary, Villa Guardamunt, St Moritz, 1918–19
London £45,000 ($92,250). 24.VII.79
From the collection of the Nijinsky estate

The autograph manuscript of Nijinsky's diary contains approximately 30,000 words of unpublished material and fifteen pages of dance notation in addition to the text first published in 1937. It is a remarkable document as a record of the dancer's life and a witness to the state of mind of a creative genius near to madness. As he became increasingly disturbed, Nijinsky turned more and more to his diary, and, according to his wife, Romola, wrote 'feverishly for hours, day and night'. Finally, in the spring of 1919, his mind gave way and he lapsed into insanity, a state from which he never fully recovered

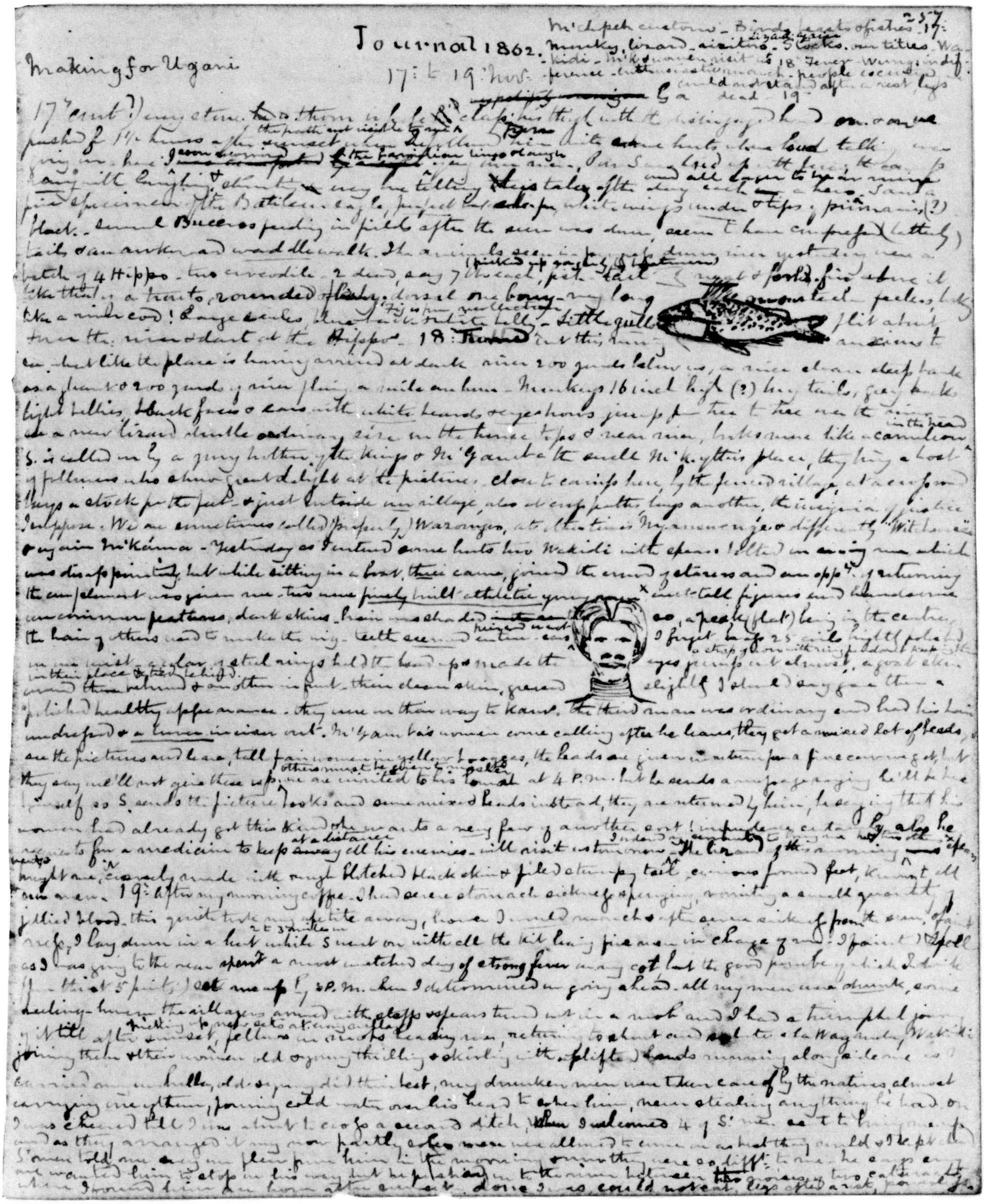

Journal 1862

Making for Ugani

JAMES AUGUSTUS GRANT
The autograph journal of his journey across Central Africa with John Hanning Speke in search
of the source of the Nile, 1860–63
London £36,000 ($73,800). 13.III.79

WOLFGANG AMADEUS MOZART
An autograph letter to his father, Vienna, 4 April 1787
New York $47,000 (£22,927). 28.XI.78

GENERAL SIR EYRE COOTE, KB
The papers, journals, letter and order books relating to his
military expeditions, 1776–1815
London £30,000 ($61,500). 13.III.79

JOHN GALSWORTHY, OM
The archive of his literary manuscripts, diaries
and letters, 1904–32
London £48,000 ($98,400). 24.VII.79
From the collection of the John Galsworthy estate

General Sir Eyre Coote fought in the American War of
Independence and was taken prisoner at Yorktown. He
subsequently served in the West Indies, and for his services was
made aide-de-camp to the King. In 1798 he was given the
important command of Dover and during the Napoleonic wars he
fought both in the Netherlands and the Mediterranean area

Fig 1
JAMES I
The coloured initial letter portrait of James I from a royal letters patent in favour of Meriel
'Littleton' restoring her late husband's estates and reversing the attainder in favour of their
children, on vellum with the Great Seal of England, 17 June 1603
London £4,500 ($9,225). 12.XII.78

The Lytteltons of Hagley Hall

Geoffrey Beard

The Lyttelton papers are a chronicle of one family's contribution to English life, mixing personal detail with political importance, and stretching back as far as the reign of King John (Fig 3) when they lived in the parish of Littelton, Worcestershire. In 1476 they acquired the manor of Frankley and resided there until Sir John Lyttelton purchased the adjacent domain of Hagley in 1564.

At the beginning of the seventeenth century Sir John's grandson and namesake brought disgrace on the family by implicating himself in the Earl of Essex's rebellion. Although reprieved from sentence of death he died in prison and left to his wife, Meriel, the sole care of their children. She reared them in the Protestant faith contrary to the family's previous tradition of Catholicism. Regarded as the saviour of the family, she obtained a grant from James I (Fig 1) restoring her late husband's forfeited estates and reversing the attainder in favour of their children. The superb coloured initial letter portrait on this document is of great rarity.

One Lyttelton was numbered among the Gunpowder Plot conspirators, but during the Civil War the family were active in the Royalist cause. Sir Thomas and his son, Henry, were imprisoned by Cromwell, and another son, Charles, was twice compelled to flee to France. Among the Lyttelton papers are many documents signed by Charles I and II appointing the Lytteltons to military and official positions (Fig 2). When William, Prince of Orange was marching towards London in 1688 both Henry and Charles remained faithful to James II.

In the eighteenth century the central figure was George, dubbed by contemporaries 'the good Lord Lyttelton'. He was born in 1709 in the house that Horace Walpole described as being 'immeasurably bad and old'. It is to George that we owe the building of the new Hagley Hall in 1754–60 and the important landscaping of the park. The house was designed by his architect friend, Sanderson Miller of Radway, and in the grounds were set urns and temples, including James Stuart's first attempt in England at the Greek revival style (1758). The undulating hills and valleys of the estate give variety to the surrounding landscape which is backed by the distant Malverns.

As an author of note himself, George attracted the friendship of many poets and scholars. James Thomson and a host of other literati stayed at Hagley. The edition of 1744 of *The Seasons* may have been revised there and his visits were commemorated in

Fig 2
CHARLES I
Royal letters patent appointing Sir Thomas 'Littleton' and others as
commissioners of array for the city of Worcester, on vellum with the
Great Seal of England, 14 September 1642
London £800 ($1,640). 12.XII.78

Fig 3
KING JOHN
Royal letters patent granting to the Abbey of Halesowen the Manor of
Hales, on vellum with the Great Seal of England, 8 August 1215
London £6,000 ($12,300). 12.XII.78

lines added to *Spring*. Horace Walpole was also a frequent guest (Fig 4), and in August 1753, ten years after Thomson had recorded its more or less natural state, Walpole enthused over the changes: 'I wore out my eyes with gazing, my feet with climbing, and my tongue and vocabulary with commending'. George was also a politician and, somewhat surprisingly, became Chancellor of the Exchequer.

His literary and political circle, together with the acquaintances of his brothers, gave great variety and richness to the papers. William Henry, was for many years Governor of South Carolina and also of Jamaica, and from the former appointment remain important letter books concerning relations with the American Indians between 1757 and 1760. Charles, the third of the six brothers, was Bishop of Carlisle and a president of the Society of Antiquaries. Among the papers of their illegitimate brother, Admiral Thomas Smith, who presided at the trial of Admiral Byng, are many comments on contemporary conditions in the Navy as well as a rare letter from Richard Wilson some months after his arrival in Italy (Fig 5).

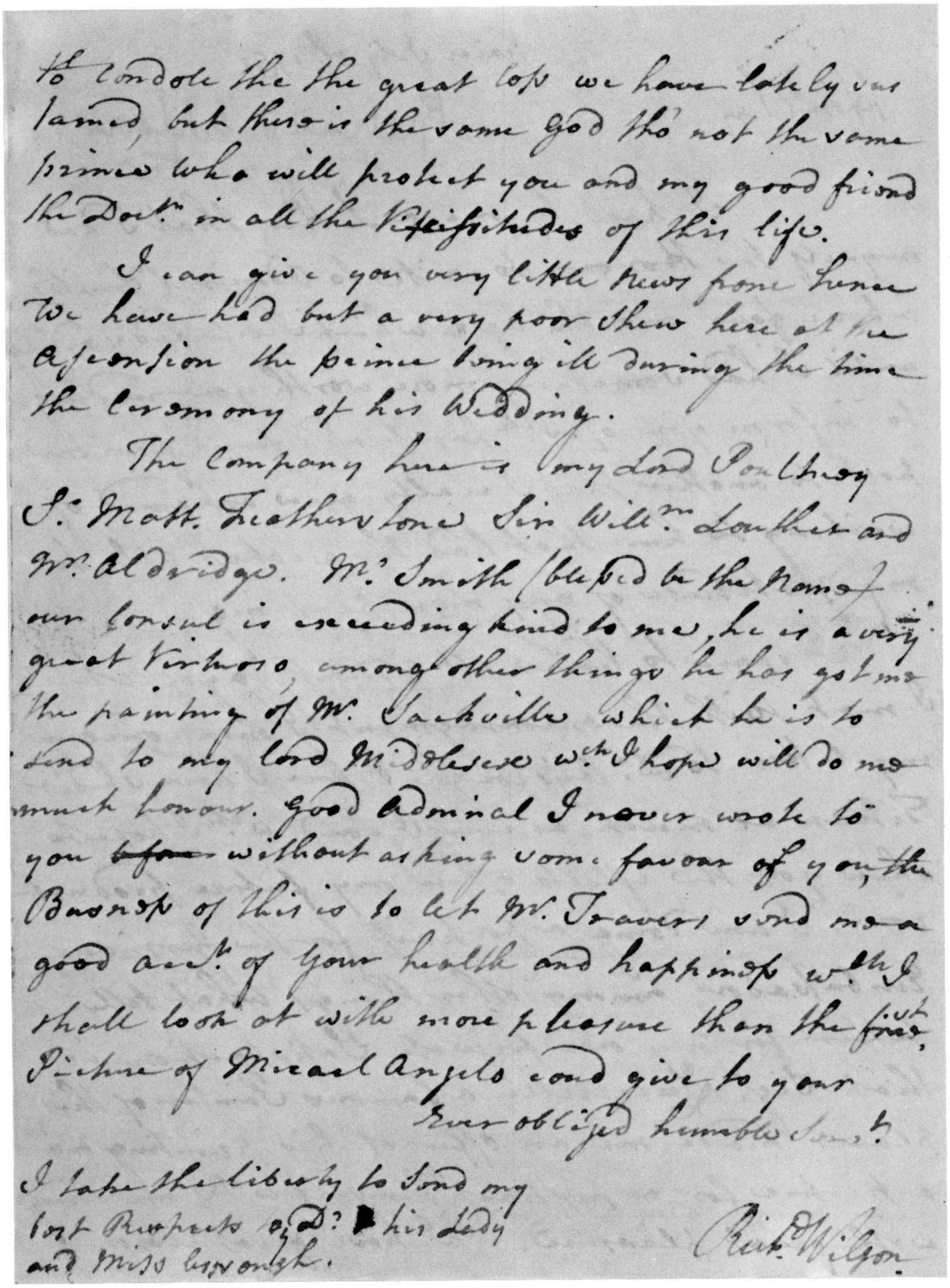

Fig 5
RICHARD WILSON
An autograph letter to Admiral Thomas Smith describing his work and studies in Venice,
8 June 1751
London £400 ($820). 12.XII.78

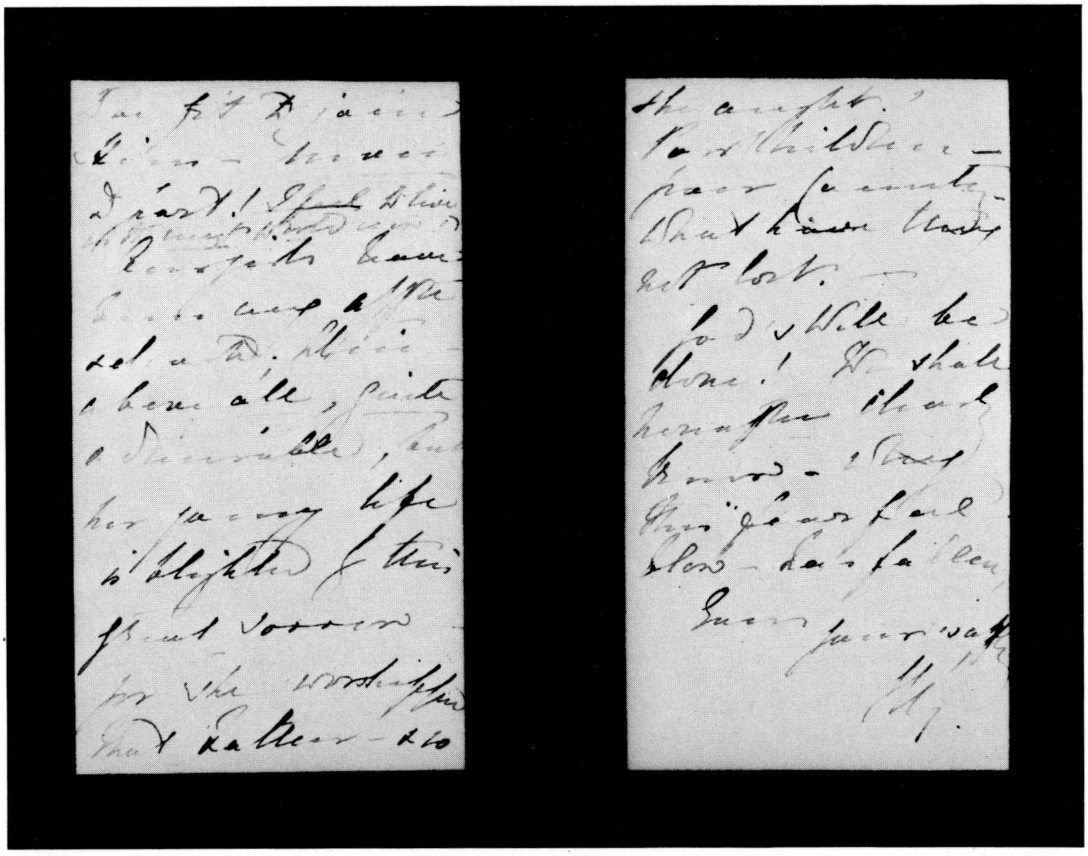

Fig 6
QUEEN VICTORIA
An autograph letter to Lady Sarah Lyttleton, written soon after the death of the Prince Consort,
29 January 1862
London £1,900 ($3,895). 12.XII.78

The 4th Baron Lyttelton (1817–76) was a dedicated educationalist, brother-in-law of W. E. Gladstone (who appears in the papers in the unlikely guise of a poet) and a colonial administrator of distinction in New Zealand. He also continued the traditions of literary friendships, and of batting with his cricket-loving brothers on wet days in Hagley's Long Gallery! He corresponded with Charles Dickens on prostitution in the theatre, with Thomas Carlyle about the London Library, with Cardinal Newman at the time of his conversion to the Catholic church, and with many other well-known figures. His mother, Lady Sarah Lyttelton, had been governess to Queen Victoria's children between 1840 and 1861 and from this period survive sixty-two autograph letters from the Queen. These include detailed instructions about the children's upbringing as well as comments on important issues of the day. One, written soon after Albert's death, describes her extreme sense of loss (Fig 6).

The above papers were part of a large heritage much of which remains in Hagley Hall. The house, now refurbished, has recently been opened to the public and a number of the papers retained by the family are on permanent display there.

EDWARD THOMAS
Fifty-seven autograph letters to his friend and fellow
poet John Freeman during the period from Thomas's
emergence as a poet to five days before his death at
the Front, 1909–17
London £10,000 ($20,500). 24.VII.79

THE REVEREND ROBERT FRANCIS KILVERT
The autograph manuscript of one volume of his diary,
27 April to 10 June 1870
London £10,500 ($21,525). 24.VII.79

WILLIAM HENRY HARRISON
A printed document signed by the President six days
before his death, Philadelphia, 29 March 1841
New York $22,000 (£10,732). 30.I.79
From the collection of Nathaniel E. Stein

ABRAHAM LINCOLN
An autograph letter to General Grant
requesting a position in the army for
his son, Robert Todd Lincoln,
Washington DC, 19 January 1865
New York $32,000 (£15,610). 14.XI.78

Below
JOHN F. KENNEDY
An autograph quotation from his
inaugural address on 20 January 1961,
signed and dated *August 1961*
New York $17,000 (£8,293). 14.XI.78

Right **GEORGE WASHINGTON**
The autograph plan for the order of battle for the
Light Infantry under Lafayette's command at the
Battle of Peekskill, 1 August 1780
New York $28,000 (£13,659). 20.VI.79

The documents on this page are from the collection
of the Elsie O. and Philip D. Sang Foundation

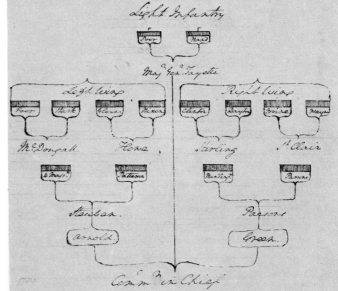

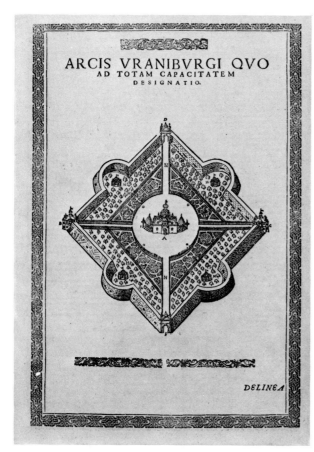

TYCHO BRAHE
Astronomiae instaurate Mechanica, first edition,
Wandesbeck, 1598
£16,000 ($32,800)

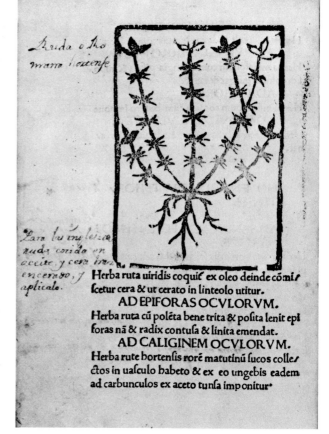

APULEIUS BARBARUS
Herbarum, first edition, Joannes Philippus de Lignamine,
Rome, 1483–84(?)
£7,000 ($14,350)

This is the first printed herbal and contains the first
series of plant illustrations ever published. It is a very
uncommon book, not only must it have been much used
but the original edition was probably in the order of only
125 to 150 copies.

CHRISTOPHER FABIUS BRECHTEL
Nomenclatura pharmaceutica, Sebastian Heusler,
Nuremberg, 1603
£5,500 ($11,275)

These 236 leaves, printed on one side only, are titles or
labels to be cut out for use in the apothecary's shop

The books on this page are from the Honeyman Collection and were sold in London on 30 October 1978

ARISTOTLE
De Animalibus, first edition, Johannes de Colonia and Johannes Manthen, Venice, 1476
London £20,000 ($41,000). 30.X.78
From the Honeyman Collection

This book is an example of an incomplete decorated incunable, the border at the pen and ink over pencil stage, ready for illumination

Représentation des Animaux de la Ménagerie de. . . . Monseigneur le Prince Eugène François (Prince of
Savoy), engraved title page and twelve plates, 1734, bound with four other works
London £8,000 ($16,400). 26.III.79

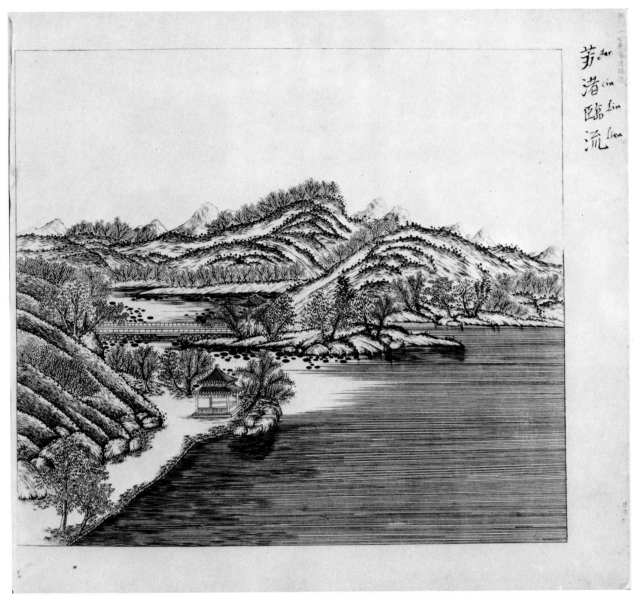

MATTEO RIPA
Views of the Chinese Imperial palaces and gardens in Jehol, Manchuria, thirty-two plates from the first
edition of the first engraved plates printed in China, 1713
London £11,000 ($22,550). 17.X.78

Only nine sets of these engravings are recorded

A selection of the duplicate books from the library at Longleat House, Wiltshire
London £322,865 ($661,873). 11.VI.79

Opposite
NICOLAUS JOSEPHUS JACQUIN
Selectarum Stirpium Americanarum Historia, a book of 264 watercolours of plants with a watercolour
and gouache title page by Franz Bauer and an inscription from Jacquin to Madame la Comtesse du
Nord, Vienna, 1780–81
London £36,000 ($73,800). 2.VII.79

This title was specially painted for Maria Feodorovna, wife of Paul I, Emperor of Russia. Paul and his
wife made a European tour in 1781–82 travelling under the assumed names 'Comte et Comtesse du
Nord'. Only twelve to eighteen copies of this de luxe edition were produced

Papaver Orientale.

EDWARD ORME
Collection of British Field Sports, first edition, twenty hand-coloured aquatint plates after Samuel
Howitt, 1807 – 1808
London £17,000 ($34,850). 14.V.79

Opposite
BALDASSARRE CATTRANI
Papaver orientale, primula maxima, twenty drawings depicting specimens for the botanical garden at
Padua, 1806
Florence L 27,000,000 (£15,341:$31,449). 14.XI.78

EDWARD GORDON CRAIG
Book of Penny Toys, 43 illustrations by the author,
one of 550 copies, Hackbridge, 1899
Hodgson's Rooms £380 ($779). 7.VI.79

M. V. WHEELHOUSE
The complete series of eight watercolour
drawings to illustrate *We and the World*
by Juliana Horatia Ewing, each signed
and dated *'09*
Hodgson's Rooms £680 ($1,394). 6.IV.79

Fairburn's New London Conjuror, circa 1815
Hodgson's Rooms £650 ($1,333). 6.VII.79
From the collection of Dr D. W. Findlay

BEATRIX POTTER
Watercolour studies of mice, dated *Oct '90*
Hodgson's Rooms £900 ($1,845). 6.IV.79
From the collection of Joy E. Collamore

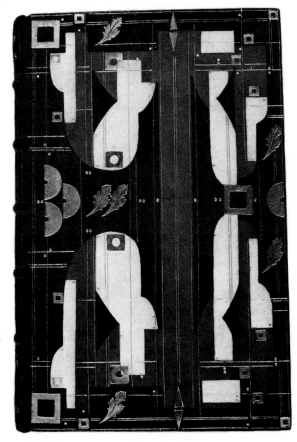

JOHN KEATS
Poems, wood-engraved borders and initials by
Charles Ricketts, two volumes, Vale Press, 1898,
bound by Sybil Pye in dark green morocco with
elaborate design on covers composed of light brown
morocco and cream pigskin onlays with gilt line
tooling, signed with monogram and dated *1922*
Hodgson's Rooms £2,400 ($4,920). 22.III.79

FREDERICK WILLIAM ROLFE (Baron Corvo)
Tarcissus, the Boy Martyr of Rome, first
edition, Saffron Walden, 1880
Hodgson's Rooms £900 ($1,845). 20.VII.79

KAY NIELSEN
Slave, an ink, pencil and watercolour costume design
for *Aladdin* written by Adam Ohlenschläger and
produced by Johannes Poulsen, Copenhagen, 1918
Hodgson's Rooms £780 ($1,599). 27.X.78
From the collection of Mrs Poulson Skou

W. HEATH ROBINSON
The Magnetic Trench Clearer, an ink and wash
drawing, signed, *circa* 1915
Hodgson's Rooms £360 ($738). 23.III.79
From the collection of Giles Bird

DAVID ROBERTS
*The Holy Land, Syria, Idumea, Arabia, Egypt
and Nubia*, six volumes, subscriber's proof
copy with hand-coloured and mounted
plates, 1842–49
Hodgson's Rooms £31,000 ($63,550). 29.VI.79

GEORGE BARBIER
Les Chansons de Bilitis by Pierre Louys, bound by
F. L. Schmied after a design by George Barbier, blue and
green morocco with black and grey morocco onlays and
gilt tooling, Pierre Corrard, Paris, 1922
Hodgson's Rooms £1,500 ($3,075). 23.II.79

CUSIN, monstre à double aile, au mufle Elephantin,
Canal à tirer sang, qui voletant en presse
Sifles d'un son aigu, ne picque ma Maistresse,
Et la laisse dormir du soir jusqu'au matin.

90

HENRI MATISSE
Florilège des Amours by Pierre de Ronsard, one of twenty
copies signed by the artist and published with extra
lithographs, Albert Skira, Paris, 1948
Hodgson's Rooms £6,100 ($12,505). 23.II.79
From the collection of Madame Jean Matisse

Le feu

GEORGE BARBIER
*Falbalas et Fanfreluches: Almanach des Modes Présentes,
Passées et Futures*, five volumes, Jules Meynial, Paris,
1922–26
Hodgson's Rooms £1,250 ($2,563). 22.II.79

GREGORIO LAMBRANZI
Neue und Curieuse Theatralische Tanz-Schul, first edition, 101 plates with musical headpieces and descriptions of each dance, Georg Puschner, Nuremberg, 1716
London £6,200 ($12,710). 17.VII.79
From the collection of John David Gray; formerly in the collection of Jack Cole

Musical Instruments

A two-manual harpsichord by Jacob Kirckman, inscribed on the nameboard *Jacobus Kirckman Londini fecit 1767*, length 7ft 9in (236.5cm)
New York $50,000 (£24,390). 26.VI.79

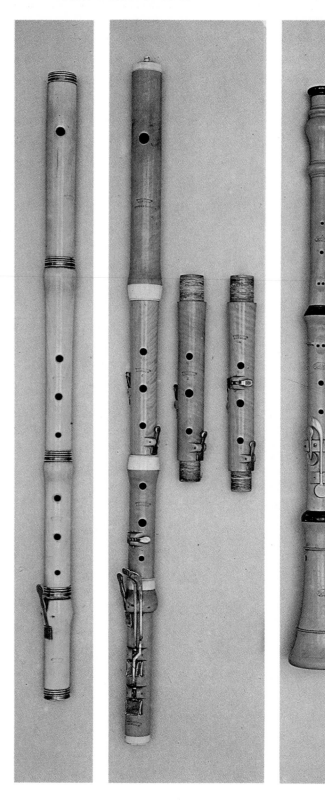

From left to right
A one-keyed ivory flute by Thomas Stanesby Junior, London, stamped *Stanesby Iunior*, 1725–50, sounding length 21¾in (55.2cm)
London £5,200 ($10,660). 6.III.79

A six-keyed boxwood flute by William Milhouse, stamped *W. Milhouse, London, 337 Oxford Stt*, sounding lengths with each joint 23⅛in (58.7cm), 23 7/16 in (59.2cm), 23¾in (60.3cm)
London £1,050 ($2,153). 6.III.79

A two-keyed oboe by the Noblet brothers, Paris, stamped *Noblet Frères, circa* 1800, length 22¼in (56.5cm)
London £1,100 ($2,255). 6.III.79

The Ebersholt violin by Joseph Guarneri del Jesu, Cremona, 1739, labelled *Joseph Guarnerius fecit Cremonae Anno 1739*, length of back 13$\frac{7}{8}$in (35.3cm) London £112,000 ($229,600). 8.XI.78
From the collection of Yehudi Menuhin

A violin by Joseph filius Andrea Guarneri, Cremona, 1703, labelled *Josephus filius Andrea Guarnerius fecit Cremonae, sub titulo S. Teresiae 1703*, length of back 13$\frac{15}{16}$in (35.4cm)
London £45,000 ($92,250). 8.XI.78

Two views of the Gore-Booth, ex Baron Rothschild, violoncello by Antonio Stradivari, Cremona, 1710, labelled *Antonius Stradivarius Cremonensis faciebat anno 1710*, length of back $29\frac{13}{16}$in (75.8cm) London £145,000($297,250). 9.XI.78

The Gore-Booth Stradivari violoncello

Peter Biddulph

Antonio Stradivari was undisputably the finest stringed instrument maker of his day and two and a half centuries later he remains unsurpassed as an innovator in construction and design. This is especially true of his 'cellos, and the Gore-Booth, made in his sixty-sixth year, illustrates perfectly the form he finally attained.

The design of the violoncello had been in question since its conception during the second part of the sixteenth century. The early makers could not decide on its dimensions, or even the number of strings. However, with the founding of the Cremonese School, Andrea Amati and his two sons Antonio and Hieronymous, began to make 'cellos more or less as we know them today, though invariably constructed on a larger model. Their use at this time (1540–1630) was almost certainly confined to providing a bass line for church music as no solo music is known to have been written for the 'cello prior to 1630. Nicolo Amati, son of Hieronymous, carried on the Cremonese tradition and set up a workshop that became famous throughout Europe. Here, first as a pupil and later assistant to Nicolo Amati, Antonio Stradivari began to find his genius.

Although Stradivari experimented with the design of the violin, when making 'cellos he preferred to follow the traditions of his teacher and from 1680 to 1701 he used a large model. Meanwhile, his contemporaries, Andrea Guarneri, Francesco Rugieri and Giovanni Battista Rogeri, all pupils of Nicolo Amati, were already making smaller 'cellos, no doubt influenced by the new generation of players who were finding the larger instrument unsuitable for solo music.

During 1709–12 Stradivari was experimenting more than ever with violin proportions and not surprisingly, he turned his attention to developing a more beautifully proportioned 'cello. Although he had produced his first smaller 'cello in 1707, the Gore-Booth of 1710 was the first truly great 'cello that Stradivari built on these new dimensions. There are other even more notable examples, such as the Duport (1711), the Batta (1714), and the Piatti (1720), but none of these instruments differs in concept from the Gore-Booth. Indeed, the solution must have been popular, Stradivari did not depart from these measurements for at least twenty years and then only to make an even smaller 'cello.

Time has shown the correctness of his judgement as no subsequent maker has produced a more perfect sounding 'cello than the type represented by the Gore-Booth. Today we can only marvel at his genius in utilising the principle of the Golden Mean to create an instrument that is not only practical but of extraordinary beauty.

Two views of the Hubermann, ex Kreisler, violin by Antonio Stradivari, Cremona, 1733, labelled
Antonius Stradivarius Cremonensis faciebat Anno 1733, length of back 14in (35.6cm)
London £145,000 ($297,250). 3.V.79
From the collection of the late Daniel Tschudi

From left to right
A chased gold-mounted violin bow by James Tubbs,
London, stamped *Jas Tubbs*, engraved on the ferrule
Leeds College of Music Xmas 1897 awarded to A.W. Kaye,
weight 58grams
London £3,200 ($6,560). 3.V.79
From the collection of Vincent Howard

A gold and ivory-mounted violin bow, the ex Baron
de Tremont, by François Tourte, Paris, 1780–90,
weight 64.5grams
New York $19,000 (£9,268). 1.XII.78

A gold and tortoiseshell-mounted violin bow by François
Tourte, Paris, *circa* 1815, weight 60grams
London £11,000 ($22,550). 8.XI.78

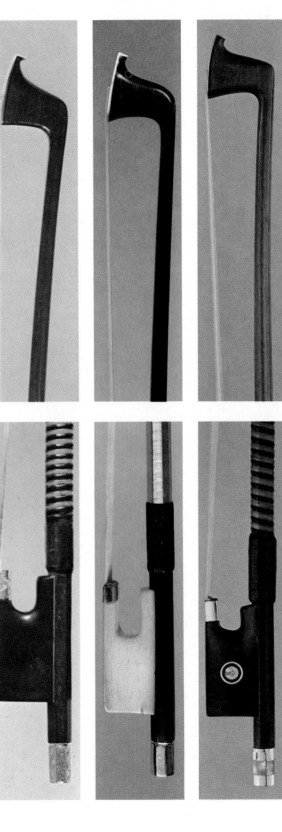

The Carl Flesch, ex Duc de Campo-Selice, violin by
Peter Guarneri of Venice, 1747, labelled *Petrus
Guarnerius filius Joseph Cremonensis fecit Venetijs
1747*, length of back $13\frac{15}{16}$in (35.4cm)
London £45,000 ($92,250). 3.V.79
From the collection of the late Daniel Tschudi

A violin by Joannes Baptista Guadagnini, Piacenza,
1748, labelled *Joannes Baptista filius Laurentii
Guadagnini fecit Placentiae 1748*, length of back
14in (35.6cm)
London £45,000 ($92,250). 8.XI.78
From the collection of C.E. Horton OBE

Furniture, Decorations and Textiles

A Queen Anne burr walnut estate table, *circa* 1710, width 2ft 11½in (90cm)
New York $26,000 (£12,683). 9.VI.79
From the collection of the late Benjamin Sonnenberg

One of a set of twenty George II red-japanned chairs attributed to Giles Grendey, *circa* 1730
Britwell House £92,000 ($188,600). 20.III.79
From the collection of David and the Lady Pamela Hicks

A George II walnut-veneered chair, *circa* 1725
London £4,200 ($8,610). 11.V.79
From the collection of the late Frederick Poke

A Windsor Gothic yew, elm and beechwood triple-back settee, 1750–1800, width 5ft 5in (165cm)
New York $20,000 (£9,756). 9.VI.79
From the collection of the late Benjamin Sonnenberg

A George III mahogany rent table, *circa* 1760, diameter 4ft 7in (140cm)
New York $32,000(£15,610). 9.VI.79
From the collection of the late Benjamin Sonnenberg

A George II walnut writing table attributed to William Vile, *circa* 1740, width 5ft 9½in (177cm)
New York $40,000 (£19,512). 9.VI.79
From the collection of the late Benjamin Sonnenberg

A George I burr walnut bureau on stand, *circa* 1725, width 1ft 9½in (54.5cm)
London £8,800 ($18,040). 22.VI.79
From the collection of Mr and Mrs Alex Abrahams

Fig 1
A George I parcel-gilt burr walnut bureau cabinet in the manner of Giles Grendey,
circa 1725, height 8ft 3in (251.5cm)
London £30,000 ($61,500). 1.XII.78

English furniture from the Hochschild Collection

Christopher Gilbert

Gerald Hochschild, a member of the Chilean mining family, acquired the majority of his collection over the last fifteen years, mainly through the London trade. The pieces furnished his house in Cheyne Walk and later a Parisian residence – a renowned collection which during its short life was talked about more than seen.

Many important pieces came from famous country houses such as Tyttenhanger Park, Elvaston Castle, Combe Abbey, Croome Court, Hornby Castle, Arundel Castle, Kedleston Hall, Harewood House, Madingley Hall, Hinton House and Woburn Abbey. One significant provenance can be added: the lively pair of rococo wall brackets incorporating chinoiserie dragons (lot 47) came originally from Newburgh Priory, Yorkshire, and belonged to a key group of festive carved and gilt furniture based on Thomas Johnson's published designs. In view of the accredited ancestry of so many fine works it is perhaps a little surprising that the authorship of only two pieces is securely supported by documentation, the pair of ormolu-mounted Derbyshire Spar ewers supplied by Matthew Boulton to the Earl of Sefton in 1772 for £14.14.00 and a celebrated black and gold lacquer dressing commode commissioned by Edwin Lascelles from Thomas Chippendale for the state bedchamber at Harewood House in 1773 at a cost of £30. Naturally, speculative attributions made on the basis of stylistic analogy with the proven work of eminent London cabinet-makers such as Grendey, Goodison, Gordon, Channon, Linnell, Ince and Mayhew and Norman abound in the sale catalogue. Hopefully, the investigation of relevant estate archives will eventually confirm some of these ascriptions.

The principal theme of Hochschild's collection was clearly English eighteenth-century furniture, particularly early gilt gesso work and furniture of Chippendale's *Director* period. He showed less enthusiasm for neo-classical creations. There is, however, evidence of a taste for flamboyant Regency decorative art, perhaps an off-shoot of his passion for oriental finery expressed by the presence of genuine Chinese lacquer work, wallpapers, pottery and bronzes, together with various English examples of chinoiserie. Interesting sub-groups included a charming array of needle-work panels, straw work, marble slabs and refined ormolu. Although, as in even the best museum holdings, there were a few 'rogues' and over-restored specimens, Hochschild obviously had a keen eye for quality and was fussy about condition.

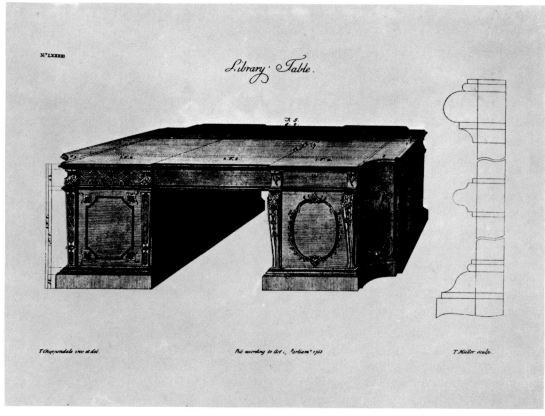

Fig 2
A plate from *The Gentleman and Cabinet-maker's Director* by Thomas Chippendale, to which the design of the Combe Abbey library table corresponds

The most spectacular piece in the collection, unquestionably one of the truly great examples of English furniture, was a majestic library writing table from Combe Abbey (Fig 3) which had descended in Lord Craven's family until sold at Sotheby's by the Countess of Craven precisely seventeen years earlier to the day. It was then acquired by a consortium of three dealers and languished in the trade for several years before Hochschild bought it, reputedly for £16,000.

There are arguably only four classic mid-Georgian library tables: the monumental Gothic example ordered by the Earl and Countess of Pomfret for Pomfret Castle, Arlington Street about 1758–60, now at Temple Newsam House, Leeds; the richly carved mahogany desk supplied by Thomas Chippendale to Sir Rowland Winn in 1766 at a cost of £72.10.00 (possibly the most distinguished) which remains in the library at Nostell Priory together with its full supporting cast of chairs, library steps, artist's table and medal cabinet; the lavish marquetry table from Harewood, now also at Temple Newsam and the Combe Abbey library table which is deservedly one of the relatively few named pieces of English furniture.

The design corresponds to the right-hand side of a plate in the first (1754) edition of Chippendale's celebrated pattern book *The Gentleman and Cabinet-maker's Director* (Fig 2), and since both the timber and cabinet work are of the highest quality, this table is traditionally regarded as a product of Chippendale's workshop. Unfortunately, in the absence of relevant documentation there is no definitive proof that it was made under Chippendale's supervision. He is certainly known to have supplied furniture quoting designs published in his pattern book, but it is prudent to remember that on at least two occasions Chippendale's patrons commissioned rival firms to provide furniture based on *Director* designs, so the only unambiguous evidence for his authorship is to trace the original bill. A search of the Combe Abbey papers might be rewarded by such a discovery. Meanwhile, the library table is no less memorable because its maker remains to be identified.

Another piece related to, although not exactly translating, one of Chippendale's *Director* designs, was an extraordinary walnut commode clothes-press with a *bombé* lower stage (Fig 5). The well figured quarter-cut veneers and strange carved rococo ornament invest the countenance with a weird personality which either attracts or perplexes connoisseurs: it is impossible to preserve a neutral attitude towards this powerful creation. The old-fashioned choice of walnut for such a progressive design suggests that it was either an early model before *The Director* was published which

Fig 3
The Combe Abbey library table attributed to Thomas Chippendale, mahogany, *circa* 1755, width 8ft 1in (246.5cm)
London £100,000($205,000). 1.XII.78

possibly inspired Chippendale's engraving, or was the product of a continental workshop. Today we can only trace its origins back to an unidentified country-house sale just after World War II, when it was bought by the late Herbert Laycock of Skipton. He was so fond of it that he steadfastly refused to sell and it was only after his death that the press came on the market again.

Three distinguished pieces derive from the famous collection of the Dukes of Leeds at Hornby Castle, Yorkshire, mostly dispersed in 1930: a prodigious carved and gilt rococo chandelier; a sumptuous mahogany wine cooler, embellished with brass-gilt mounts in the neo-classical taste and a towering early eighteenth-century pier glass sporting an elaborate fronded cresting (Fig 7). The latter was presumably commissioned either for the 1st Duke's palatial residence at Wimbledon, or Kiveton, his country seat in Yorkshire, both of which were being equipped in the highest style of elegance during the early eighteenth century. The Kiveton inventory of 1727 records many conspicuously grand looking glasses which may relate to this example.

An imposing parcel-gilt burr walnut bureau cabinet with a *bombé* lower stage and smart gilt corner mounts aroused a good deal of interest at the sale (Fig 1). The doors, framing shaped mirror plates and a Palladian pediment, relate to a well-known group of mahogany cabinets associated on the evidence of labelled examples with Giles Grendey of London. The *bombé* base, however, is reminiscent of continental fashions. The fact that the secretaire came to light in Copenhagen may be significant, since

Fig 4
A George II brass-inlaid mahogany table attributed to John Channon, *circa* 1740, width 2ft 9½in (85cm)
London £14,000 ($28,700). 1.XII.78

Opposite
Fig 5
A George II walnut commode clothes-press attributed to Thomas Chippendale, *circa* 1755, height 5ft 5in (165cm)
London £22,000 ($45,100). 1.XII.78

Grendey is known to have shipped large consignments to Scandinavia and further-more, regularly styled his export furniture to appeal to the tastes of foreign cus-tomers. Thus, the intriguing possibility exists that we have here an example of London-made cabinet furniture specially designed for the export trade.

The Hochschild Collection also included a refined mahogany occasional table delicately inlaid with engraved brass patterns, one of the elements bearing the crest of the Marsh family (Fig 4). This graceful table belongs to an uncommonly interesting group within the family of high quality brass-inlaid furniture dating from the 1740s which John Hayward attributes to John Channon's workshop on the strength of stylistic affinities with a signed pair of bookcases at Powderham Castle, Devon. Brass inlay is normally associated with the Regency period, and although some wisps of mystery remain it seems likely that John Channon of St Martin's Lane was the only London cabinet-maker employing this decorative technique in the 1740s. This sleek little table, although in a minor key, is an outstanding specimen of English craftsman-ship and restrained good taste.

Fig 6
A George III black and gold lacquer commode by Thomas Chippendale, 1773, width 5ft 4in (162.5cm)
London £52,000 ($106,600). 1.XII.78

Fig 7
A Queen Anne giltwood pier glass,
circa 1705, height 8ft 4in (254cm).
London £8,000 ($16,400). 1.XII.78

A piece of furniture which could go straight into any museum in the world was a handsome black and gold lacquer breakfront dressing commode made by Thomas Chippendale for the state bedchamber at Harewood House, Yorkshire, and invoiced on 12 November 1773 as 'A large Commode with folding Doors vaneer'd with your own Japann with additions Japann'd to match with a dressing Drawer & fine locks £30' (Fig 6). It was provided with a damask leather cover to protect the luxurious top from damage. The technique of veneering cabinets with Oriental lacquer was favoured by French *ébénistes* but only rarely employed in England where patrons were expected to supply their own facing panels to the cabinet-maker. The massive dignity, repose and sheer opulence of this commode render it the most illustrious piece in the collection and stamp it as a masterpiece of English cabinet-making.

A George II brass-inlaid mahogany bureau bookcase in the manner of John Channon, *circa* 1740, height 7ft 2in (219cm)
New York $19,000 (£9,268). 17.II.79

A George III painted cabinet, the doors repainted in the style of Boucher, *circa* 1765,
height 5ft 8in (173cm)
London £6,200 ($12,710). 22.VI.79
From the collection of Mr and Mrs Alex Abrahams

A Queen Anne mahogany block-front desk, Massachusetts, *circa* 1750, width 3ft (91.5cm)
New York $50,000 (£24,390). 3.II.79
From the collection of Mr and Mrs Richard Titelman

A Chippendale mahogany block-front kneehole dressing table, Boston, *circa* 1770, width 2ft 11¼in (89.5cm)
New York $41,000(£20,000). 23.VI.79

Three pieces from an American laminated rosewood parlour suite attributed to John and
Joseph W. Meeks, New York, *circa* 1860
PB Eighty-four $19,000 (£9,268). 14.II.79

American rococo revival furniture

John Block

By the 1840s the rococo revival had arrived in America brought by cabinet-makers who had received their initial training in Europe during the early nineteenth century. Throughout the 1850s and '60s artisans, such as the German-born John Henry Belter and Joseph W. Meeks in New York, were producing large quantities of intricately carved furniture based on early eighteenth-century French curvilinear designs.

The pieces most in demand were those carved with naturalistic floral, fruit and vine motifs. The wood was laminated for greater pliability and durability, thus enabling it to be bent and carved to the Victorian cabinet-makers' often innovative designs – the eighteenth-century models were adapted to suit American taste as well as new machine production methods. Rosewood was one of the most popular materials with buyers of the day and also one of the most suitable for lamination.

The last year has seen confirmation of the growing interest in this style of furniture as a collector's item and it is the same kind of pieces that are sought after. A table by Belter of laminated rosewood with a serpentine white marble top brought $8,000 (£3,902) after active bidding by buyers from throughout America.

Perhaps the most interesting example to have appeared in the salerooms was a parlour suite thought to have been made in New York, *circa* 1860, by John and Joseph W. Meeks (see opposite). Using the Belter process of laminating rosewood, Meeks created a gentleman's chair, four side chairs and a settee that seem to be sculptural works of art rather than simply a group of furniture. The pierced-carved crestrails incorporating flowers, grape clusters and scrolling vines, represent the epitome of this increasingly popular style.

Many other cabinet-makers also set up shops and factories in New York. During the apogee of the rococo revival, craftsmen such as Alexander Roux, Charles Baudouine and Charles Klein were producing furniture of solid walnut, rosewood, and mahogany which abounded with carved shells, floral cartouches, 'S' and 'C' curves. Accomplished makers were also working in other major American cities.

The mansions in the South built before the Civil War, the urban palaces of the newly wealthy merchants and industrialists of the mid-West and the West coast and hotels in cities as far apart as New Orleans, Denver, and San Francisco were all lavishly furnished with rococo furniture and decorations, making it the most widely accepted of the revival styles. It is not surprising, therefore, that today's collectors, dealers, and museums are seeking the fanciful designs, nostalgic qualities and sturdy construction that the best of American rococo revival furniture has to offer.

A French walnut cabinet with panelled doors depicting scenes from the parable of the Prodigal Son, probably Burgundian, late sixteenth century, height 5ft 6in (168cm)
London £7,500 ($15,375). 13.VII.79

A German walnut and fruitwood-inlaid chest, seventeenth century, width 6ft (183cm)
New York $29,000 (£14,146). 9.XII.78

A boulle commode, possibly North German, *circa* 1710, width 4ft 3in (129.5cm)
London £19,000 ($38,950). 24.XI.78

A Louis XIV marquetry *bureau mazarin*, late seventeenth century, width 3ft 7¼in (110cm)
London £10,500 ($21,525). 22.VI.79
From the collection of Mr and Mrs Alex Abrahams

A gilt-metal chandelier, Flemish or Scandinavian, mid eighteenth century, height 5ft 4in (162.5cm)
London £15,000 ($30,750). 20.IV.79

A Swiss walnut cylinder bureau bookcase in the manner of Matthias Funk, mid eighteenth century, height 7ft 8½in (235cm)
London £9,500 ($19,475). 13.VII.79

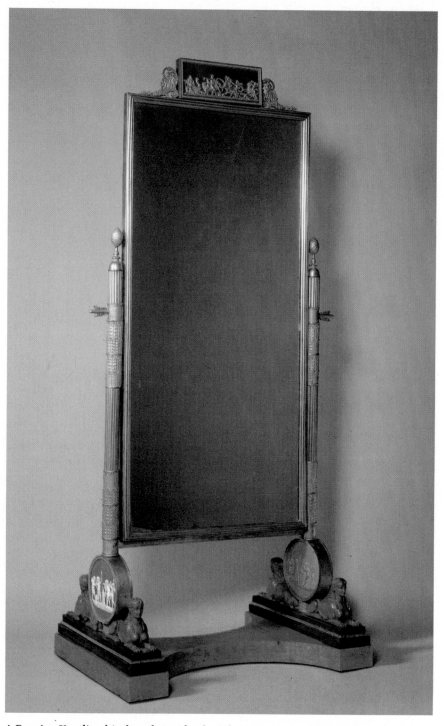

A Russian Karelian birch and ormolu cheval mirror, early nineteenth
century, height 7ft 5in (226cm)
New York $12,000 (£5,854). 10.IV.79

An ormolu-mounted amboyna *secrétaire à abattant*, early nineteenth century, height 4ft 8½in (143.5cm)
Britwell House £5,000 ($10,250). 20.III.79
From the collection of David and the Lady Pamela Hicks

One of a set of four Louis XV gilt armchairs,
mid eighteenth century
London £11,000 ($22,550). 24.XI.78

A Louis XV ormolu-mounted black lacquer
commode stamped *Delorme JME*, mid eighteenth century,
width 4ft 10in (147.5cm)
New York $60,000 (£29,268). 7.IV.79
From the collection of Antenor Patino

Adrien Delorme was received Master in 1748

A pair of Louis XV ormolu-mounted Ch'ien Lung cockerels mounted as candelabra, mid eighteenth century, height 2ft 1in (63.5cm)
London £30,000 ($61,500). 6.VII.79

A Louis XV/XVI transitional ormolu-mounted marquetry commode, *circa* 1775, width 4ft 1½in (125.7cm)
London £17,000($34,850). 6.VII.79
From the collection of Mrs R. J. Hearn

A pair of Louis XV ormolu-mounted fruitwood and purplewood marquetry work tables
attributed to Jean-Pierre Latz, mid eighteenth century, height 2ft 3½in (70cm)
New York $45,000 (£21,951). 7.IV.79

Fig 1
A Louis XIV ormolu-mounted boulle centre table, late seventeenth-early eighteenth century,
width 3ft 9in (114cm)
Monte Carlo FF 2,000,000 (£219,780:$450,549). 26.VI.79

A memorable sale of magnificent French furniture

Frances Buckland

Frederick the Great was very impressed by Paris and wrote to Voltaire, in a letter of 23 August 1750, that Berlin could not be considered its equal. He admitted that Paris was exceptional in having wealth, magnificence and good taste.[1] Fine eighteenth-century French furniture, an integral part of this taste, was unfashionable after the Revolution, and was appreciated by few collectors until 1850. It was after this date that the Rothschild family started to acquire it, thus stimulating more general interest. Certain pieces which once belonged to Baron Nathaniel de Rothschild in Vienna were outstanding in the large collection originally formed by three generations of the Wildenstein family. Since 1977 this collection had been owned by Akram Ojjeh and it was dispersed last summer in Monte Carlo.

Louis XIV was the king to whom France originally owed its position as the centre of fashion and outstanding craftsmanship. In 1662 he set up the great Manufacture des Gobelins to train French workmen and supply furniture to the royal palaces. A large Gobelins tapestry at the Château de Versailles shows the King's visit of 1667. It gives a good idea of the scope and skill of the craftsmen and some of the objects portrayed can be identified in the general inventories drawn up during Louis XIV's reign. The section listing furniture reveals the range of colourful and precious materials used in the construction of the magnificent cabinets, tables and *guéridons* of this period. The silver furniture at Versailles, described in the *Mercure Galant* of 1682, is famous although none of it survives today. Other materials used were jasper, lapis lazuli, agate, amethyst, cornelian and jade. There were many lacquered pieces, both Chinese, which were mainly black, and European, some blue, *'couleur de lapis avec feuillages d'or et d'argent'*, as well as work in *pietra dura*, tortoiseshell, marble, porphyry, marquetry of exotic woods, ebony and mother of pearl.

A table in the collection with intricate marquetry of different woods on a background of tortoiseshell, was typical of the products of the Manufacture des Gobelins (Fig 1). Although the name of Louis XIV's great *ébéniste*, André-Charles Boulle, is generally associated with veneers of tortoiseshell and brass, Professor Lunsingh Scheurleer's research has shown the importance of Pierre Gole in the development of this type of work in France. On this piece the marquetry was framed by an elaborate border of leaves and scrolls in brass and pewter. The colours were somewhat faded but it was still clear that the four panels on the sides were originally blue in imitation of lapis lazuli. Brightly coloured areas of blue or green were often horn rather than tortoiseshell, because it was more practical and cheaper.

The Grand Dauphin collected Chinese porcelain and his interest in chinoiserie made it very fashionable at the court of his father, Louis XIV. An inventory of 1757 of the Château de Meudon mentions *'un meuble de cabinet de petit point noir representant des vases de porcelaine de differentes façons'*, part of the furnishings supplied in 1699. This interest continued into the eighteenth century and an object of great rarity in the collection was an Arita porcelain shell with naturalistic gilt-bronze mounts (Fig 2). Sir Francis Watson has discovered a brief mention of a mounted shell of this unusual type in the inventory drawn up after the Duc de Bourbon's death in 1740. Also, an anonymous manuscript in the Condé archives describes the skilful copies of oriental works which the Duc ordered to be made.

On Louis XIV's death in 1715 his great grandson and heir was only five years old, and the government of France was therefore directed by a Regent, the Duc d'Orléans, until 1723. The most famous of the cabinet-makers of this early rococo period was Charles Cressent, who was trained as a sculptor and worked as *ébéniste* to the Regent. The dramatic sculptural quality of the mounts on Cressent's furniture was well demonstrated on a number of pieces attributed to him in this collection. On one of these, a commode (Fig 5), the central cartouche is filled with a type of marquetry not known in other work by Cressent – circles of light-coloured wood and brass, silvery in contrast with the heavily gilded mounts.

Undoubtedly the most spectacular piece in the collection was the great *encoignure* by Jacques Dubois (Fig 4). It is no exaggeration to say that it is breathtaking, partly on account of its massive scale. This *encoignure*, surmounted by an *étagère* and a clock, is so unusual that it is surprising that nothing is known of its history before it entered the Vienna Rothschild Collection. It has been suggested that it may be a royal piece, but Jacques Dubois was not a regular supplier of furniture to the French crown. The marquetry and the mounts entwined with foliage recall another immense piece of furniture, the combined bookcase, secretaire and cupboard by the same *ébéniste* at Waddesdon Manor, Buckinghamshire. It is the particularly elaborate and imaginative mounts, so important a part of the decoration of French furniture, which are the most striking feature. This remarkable piece of furniture is closely related to a drawing in the Musée des Arts Décoratifs, Paris, attributed to Nicolas Pineau.

An *ébéniste* who supplied furniture to at least one member of the royal family has recently become more widely known through the research of Henry Hawley. In his monograph on Jean-Pierre Latz (*Bulletin of the Cleveland Museum of Art*, Sept–Oct 1970) he discusses a pair of *encoignures*, veneered with end-cut marquetry of foliage and flowers, which were in this collection (Fig 7). They bore the brand *EU* surmounted by a crown, the mark of the Château d'Eu, which belonged to the Orléans family. These were more elaborate but similar in type to *encoignures* now in the Quirinale, Rome, which were supplied for Madame Infante, eldest daughter of Louis XV, after her marriage. The Marquis d'Argenson, in his journal filled with unpleasant comments about the court, does not express his admiration of Latz's work, he only complains that the King gives away too much expensive furniture. On 2 July 1749 he wrote, 'Madame Infante is leaving at last on 17 August . . . and posting to Lyons with sixteen carriages. . . . The King is spending great sums on giving furniture to her'.[2]

As well as Dubois and Latz, other *ébénistes*, such as Dautriche and Lhermite, made

Fig 2
A Louis XV ormolu-mounted shell pot-pourri vase in Arita porcelain, mid eighteenth century,
height 9in (23cm)
Monte Carlo FF 700,000 (£76,923:$157,692). 25.VI.79

use of decorative marquetry of foliage and flowers in dark wood on a lighter ground. Two of the more skilful were B.V.R.B. and Joseph Baumhauer. The identity of B.V.R.B. was uncertain until Jean Baroli (*Connaissance des Arts*, March 1957) revealed that he was Bernard van Risenburgh II, probably the *ébéniste* referred to in eighteenth-century sale catalogues as Bernard. Another exceptional piece of furniture, also impressive for its size as well as its quality, was the folio cabinet attributed in the Monte Carlo catalogue to van Risenburgh (Fig 8). Attention, however, was drawn to the affinity of this piece with the work of Joseph Baumhauer, who became *ébéniste privilégié du roi* sometime before 1767 and signed his work 'Joseph' between two fleurs-de-lis. The cabinet was veneered in contrasting *amaranthe* and *bois de rose*, the flowing mounts set off by carefully shaped areas of the darker wood. There is a marked resemblance between the treatment of the sides of the cabinet, end-cut marquetry of foliage and flowers, and two very similar but not identical commodes in the National Gallery, Washington. Certain elements of the mounts are the same and also occur on commodes by Joseph in the J. Paul Getty Museum, Malibu, and the Victoria and Albert Museum, London. The keyholes, however, are pierced in a different place on the mounts on the cabinet.

Fig 3
A Louis XVI tulipwood and sycamore marquetry *commode à vantaux* stamped *M. Carlin JME*, inscribed *Poirier. Md Rue St Honoré a Paris, circa* 1775, width 4ft 10in (148cm)
Monte Carlo FF 1,500,000 (£164,835:$337,912). 25.VI.79

Martin Carlin was received Master in 1766

Fig 4
A Louis XV ormolu-mounted marquetry
encoignure stamped *I. Dubois*, after a design
by Nicolas Pineau, mid eighteenth century,
height 9ft 6in (290cm)
Monte Carlo FF 7,600,000 (£835,165:$1,712,088).
25.VI.79

Jacques Dubois was received master in 1742
Now in the J. Paul Getty Museum, Malibu

Fig 5
An ormolu-mounted commode attributed to Charles Cressent, *circa* 1740, width 4ft 10in (148cm)
Monte Carlo FF1,300,000 (£142,857:$292,857). 25.VI.79

Fig 6
A Louis XVI ormolu-mounted marquetry commode stamped *J.-F. Leleu, circa 1775,*
width 4ft 10in (148cm)
Monte Carlo FF4,200,000 (£461,538:$946,154). 25.VI.79

Jean-François Leleu was received Master in 1764

Fig 7
One of a pair of Louis XV ormolu-
mounted marquetry *encoignures*
stamped *J.-P. Latz*, mid
eighteenth century,
width 2ft 9½in (85cm)
Monte Carlo FF 2,600,000
(£285,714:$585,714). 25.VI.79

Jean-Pierre Latz was received Master
before 1739

Jeanne-Antoine Poisson, Marquise de Pompadour, was an influential figure at the court of Louis XV and one of her favourite cabinet-makers, Jean-François Oeben, was appointed *ébéniste du roi* in 1754. Oeben's name is extremely rare in the royal records but at least two of his pupils later supplied furniture for members of the royal family.

Jean-François Leleu, who was trained in Oeben's atelier, produced the large and unusual commode veneered with fine marquetry in the neo-classic taste (Fig 6). It is perhaps worth noting that certain features of this piece relate to a drawing by Jean Bérain.[4] Among Leleu's patrons was the Prince de Condé, who employed him to make furniture for the Palais Bourbon, and detailed descriptions of these pieces can be found in the Condé archives. They give some idea of the vivid colours employed in the decoration of furniture in the second half of the eighteenth century, partly due to the revival of interest in pictorial marquetry. The colours used by Leleu's fellow pupil, J.-H. Riesener, can be traced in the royal records, and these included bright green, blue, pink, grey, black and white as well as brown, chestnut, fawn, yellow and olive. The furniture in the main rooms of the royal palaces had to look as splendid as possible and sometimes received rather drastic restoration. Pieces veneered with

Fig 8
A Louis XV ormolu-mounted marquetry folio cabinet attributed to Bernard van Risenburgh II,
mid eighteenth century, height 3ft 10½in (118cm)
Monte Carlo FF 2,800,000 (£307,692:$630,769). 25.VI.79

Bernard van Risenburgh II was received Master before 1730

elaborate marquetry from Riesener's atelier are known to have been vigorously scraped to renew the brilliance of colour. One of the interesting features of this commode was the way in which the mounts forming the handles of the two large drawers were so well co-ordinated with the marquetry that they continued the design. It would also probably have been possible to employ the panel of marquetry on this commode the other way up on another piece of furniture. Marquetry was a field in which Leleu was particularly skilled and he is listed as a leading *ébéniste-marqueteur* in the *Almanach Général des Marchands du Royaume*.

Another *ébéniste* linked with Oeben was Martin Carlin, a German who married Oeben's sister, Marie-Catherine, in 1759. Carlin was not ambitious or willing to take risks and worked mainly for the *marchands-merciers*. An interesting piece by him was formerly in the collection of the Earl of Mansfield and Mansfield (Fig 3). This *commode à vantaux* must have been made before 1778, as it bore an inscription in ink on the top *Poirier. Md Rue St Honoré a Paris.* Simon-Philippe Poirier, a leading *marchand-mercier* who supplied a great many furnishings to Madame du Barry, retired in 1778. When the central door of the commode was opened it revealed a series of drawers, six small, four medium and one long. All these were carefully veneered to give a three-dimensional effect: a light fillet of wood framing the top and left side, and a dark fillet framing the bottom and right side. This feature also appeared on the panel on the back of each door. Shading of this type was also used by Riesener, as were the distinctive gilt-bronze mounts of male terminal figures on the fore-corners of this commode.

Among the furniture of the Empire period, a pair of console tables was outstanding (Fig 9). Madame Ledoux-Lebard (*Inventaire Général du Musée de Versailles et des Trianons*, vol 1, 1975) has published a design by Charles Percier, from which F. H. G. Jacob Desmalter, *ébéniste* to the Emperor, made a console now at the Grand Trianon. The tables in the collection were very similar and strikingly large. The dramatic mounts were a combination of patinated- and gilt-bronze and the decorative veneer was yew, applied even to the backs of the tables and the underside of the shelves. If these tables were commissioned by Napoleon he may have shared a taste with Louis XIV. In the royal inventories the description of no 252 is, 'A table of English burr yew, with the legs of the same material . . . .'.[3]

If Frederick the Great had been in Monte Carlo in June 1979 he would certainly have found furniture to delight him and reinforce his high opinion of French eighteenth-century taste. As well as more pieces by the *ébénistes* already mentioned there were works by Molitor, Saunier, Roentgen, Topino and Cramer. There were also pieces of seat furniture, including royal *pliants* by J.-B. Séné, some fine *bronzes d'ameublement* and oriental rugs to complete the collection.

[1] 'Je n'ai point la folle présomption de croire que Berlin vaut Paris. Si les richesses, la grandeur et la magnificence font une ville aimable, nous le cédons à Paris. Si le bon goût, peut-être plus généralement répandu, se trouve dans un endroit du monde, je sais et je conviens que c'est à Paris.'

[2] 'Madame Infante part enfin le 17 août . . . et court la poste jusqu'à Lyon avec seize voitures. . . . Le roi depense beaucoup à lui donner des meubles.'

[3] 'Une table de racine d'if d'Angleterre, avec son pied de mesme. . . .'

[4] For a reproduction of this drawing see *L'Oeuvre Complet*, Paris, nd, pl 88

Fig 9
One of a pair of Empire ormolu- and bronze-mounted burr yew console tables attributed to
F.H.G. Jacob Desmalter, after a design by Charles Percier, *circa* 1805, width 4ft 2in (128cm)
Monte Carlo FF 700,000 (£76,923:$157,692). 25.VI.79

François Honoré Georges Jacob, called Jacob Desmalter, succeeded his father in 1796

A Louis XVI mahogany-veneered *bureau à gradin* stamped *J.-H.Riesener*, *circa* 1780–82, width 5ft 1¾in (157 cm)
Monte Carlo FF 240,000 (£26,374:$54,066). 11.II.79

Jean-Henri Riesener was received Master in 1768

A Louis XV *bergère à transformations* stamped *J.-B. Tilliard*, mid eighteenth century
Monte Carlo FF 160,000
(£17,582:$36,044). 11.II.79

Jean-Baptiste Tilliard was received Master in 1752

A Louis XV ormolu and ebony-veneered clock, the face signed *F. Berthoud* and the base stamped *B. Lieutaud*, mid eighteenth century, width 2ft 3½in (70cm)
Monte Carlo FF 130,000
(£14,286:$29,286). 11.II.79

Balthazar Lieutaud was received Master in 1749

One of a pair of Louis XIV ormolu-mounted parquetry commodes, early eighteenth century,
width 4ft 9⅛in (145cm)
Monte Carlo FF 500,000 (£54,945:$112,637). 12.II.79

A Louis XVI cylinder bureau stamped *C.-C. Saunier JME, circa* 1780, width 3ft 4in (102cm)
London £22,000 ($45,100). 24.XI.78

Claude-Charles Saunier was received Master in 1752

An ormolu and painted wood *jardinière, circa* 1900, height 3ft 2in (96.5cm)
Belgravia £4,800 ($9,840). 29.XI.78

One of a pair of bronze candelabra sculpted by Toussaint and cast by F. Barbedienne, dated *1850*, height 5ft 6in (167.5cm) Belgravia £12,500 ($25,625). 29.XI.78

One of four bronze and marble candelabra, mid nineteenth century, height 9ft 10in (300cm) Belgravia £40,000 ($82,000). 20.VI.79

An ormolu, purplewood and tulipwood barometer and a similar regulator in the style of
Martin Carlin signed *P. Sormani*, Paris, nineteenth century, height 7ft 4in (223cm)
PB Eighty-four $35,000 (£17,073). 14.II.79

A French ormolu-mounted kingwood commode in the style of Antoine Gaudreaux, *circa* 1870,
width 5ft 11in (180cm)
Belgravia £6,000 ($12,300). 28.III.79

A painted polychrome writing cabinet by Gualbert Saunders and William Burges, signed *Gualbert Saunders* and dated *1865*, height 9ft 2in (279.4cm) Belgravia £21,000 ($43,050). 6.XII.78

W.G. Saunders was a pupil of William Burges and they are known to have worked together in 1865, the year this cabinet was made. Relatively little is known of Saunders's furniture making, although the cabinet closely reflects Burges's work both in the architectural style and the detail of the panels

An ebonised mahogany Aesthetic cabinet by E.W. Godwin, *circa* 1869, height 8ft (244cm)
Belgravia £6,000($12,300). 6.XII.78
From the collection of C.C. Lane

In April 1869 Godwin was paid £3.3.0 for the design of an ebonised cabinet with silvered fittings to be
made by William Watt of Grafton Street for the Reverend Charlton Lane. The pierced 'keyhole'
escutcheons resemble very closely watercolour drawings for metal mounts by William Burges

A *feuilles d'aristoloche* tapestry, possibly Enghien, mid sixteenth century,
7ft 8in by 12ft (234cm by 366cm)
New York $82,500 (£40,244). 22.V.79

A late Gothic tapestry of St Julian the Hospitator, Franco-Flemish, *circa* 1525,
10ft 1in by 10ft 6in (307cm by 320cm)
New York $52,500 (£25,610). 22.V.79

A Louis XIV Savonnerie carpet by Simon Lourdet, mid seventeenth century, 18ft 6in by 12ft 6in
(563cm by 384cm)
Monte Carlo FF 800,000 (£87,912:$180,220). 12. II.79

A Bokhara *susani*, *circa* 1860, 7ft 10in by 6ft 4in (239cm by 193cm)
London £5,200 ($10,660). 10.I.79

A Kashan *Polonaise* silk and metal thread rug, late sixteenth century, 7ft 2in by 4ft 9in
(218cm by 145cm)
Monte Carlo FF300,000 (£32,967:$67,582). 25.VI.79
From the collection of Akram Ojjeh

A Kashan so-called Portuguese carpet,
circa 1600, 17ft 11in by 7ft 10in
(546cm by 239cm)
Monte Carlo FF450,000 (£49,451:$101,374).
25.VI.79
From the collection of Akram Ojjeh

An animal and tree *asmalik*, *circa* 1760, 4ft 11in by 2ft 10in (150cm by 86.5cm)
London £8,000 ($16,400). 25.IV.79

A Bokhara Tekke Turkman carpet, *circa* 1900, 10ft 5in by 6ft 11in (318cm by 211cm)
London £15,000 ($30,750). 10.I.79

An Adraskand carpet, *circa* 1830, 11ft 10in by 8ft (361cm by 244cm)
London £12,000 ($24,600). 25.IV.79

A Ravar Kerman carpet, possibly made by Ali Sefid, *circa* 1894, 18ft 7in by 10ft 11in (567cm by 333cm)
London £45,000 ($92,250). 12.X.78

An Isphahan rug, *circa* 1960, 9ft 6in by 9ft (290cm by 275cm)
New York $40,000 (£19,512). 16.XII.78

A Kazak rug, nineteenth century, 7ft 1in by 5ft 2in (216cm by 158cm)
PB Eighty-four $15,250(£7,439). 7.III.79

Antiquities, Asian and Primitive Art

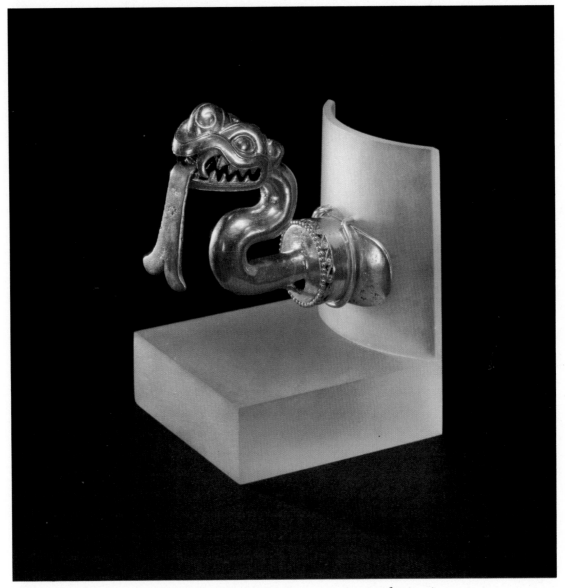

A Pre-Columbian Mixtec gold lip-plug, probably from Oaxaca, height $2\frac{3}{4}$in (7cm)
New York \$101,000 (£49,268). 22.XI.78

A Pre-Columbian Aztec wood and turquoise mask representing the god Tlaloc, 1200–1400, height 7½in (19cm)
London £23,000 ($47,150). 11.XII.78

An American Indian Pacific Northwest Coast slave
knife, height 14⅞in (37.8cm)
New York $26,000 (£12,683). 21.IV.79
From the collection of the late Robert Tyler Davis

An American Indian Eastern Woodlands wood club,
height 24⅝in (62.5cm)
London £50,000 ($102,500). 21.VI.79

An American Indian Pacific Northwest Coast wood potlatch ladle, length 19in (48.3cm)
New York $33,000 (£16,098). 21.IV.79
From the collection of the late Robert Tyler Davis

A Middle Sepik male hook figure, Sawos Area, New Guinea,
height 84in (213.4cm)
London £36,000 ($73,800). 21.VI.79

A Songo wood chief's throne, Angola, height 12⅛in (30.8cm)
London £55,000 ($112,750). 21.VI.79

A Songo wood male figure, Angola,
height 11¼in (28.5cm)
London £34,000 ($69,700). 21.VI.79

An Afro-Portuguese ivory oliphant, mid to late
sixteenth century, length 20¾in (52.7cm)
London £13,000 ($26,650). 21.VI.79

A Fang wood male reliquary figure (*bieri*), Gabon, height 17⅝in (44.8cm)
London £29,000($59,450). 11.XII.78

A Tibetan gilt-bronze standing figure of a Bodhisattva, probably Maitreya, eighteenth
century, height 53in (134.6cm)
London £6,200 ($12,710). 9.VII.79

A Moghul 'jade' bowl, inscribed and dated *AH 1022* (1613–14 AD), diameter $4\frac{3}{4}$in (12cm)
London £15,000 ($30,750). 23.IV.79
From the collection of F. W. W. Bernard

The inscription around the rim and above the foot invokes the spiritual qualities of the bowl and blesses the owner, Jahangir, son of Akbar, who commissioned the work

From left to right
An Iranian lustre pottery jug, Kashan, *circa* 1200 AD, diameter 6½in (16.5cm)
London £6,000($12,300). 10.X.78

An Iranian lustre pottery bowl, Kashan, *circa* 1200 AD, diameter 8in (20.3cm)
London £10,000($20,500). 10.X.78

An Iranian lustre pottery ewer, Kashan, *circa* 1200 AD, height 9½in (24.2cm)
London £15,000($30,750). 10.X.78

An Isnik pottery dish, 1550–1600,
diameter 10¼in (26cm)
London £8,000($16,400). 23.IV.79

Fig 1
A Roman cage-cup or *diatretum, circa* 300 AD, height 4in (10.1cm)
London £520,000 ($1,066,000). 4.VI.79

Ancient glass from the Constable-Maxwell Collection

Donald Harden

The dispersal at auction of Mr and Mrs Andrew Constable-Maxwell's collection of over 350 ancient glasses, a sale without parallel for many years past, made a vivid and lasting impression on connoisseurs and the general public. Amassed in a surprisingly short time (no more than twenty-five years), the Constable-Maxwell glasses, many superb in quality, included notable examples of near eastern glass of all periods from eighteenth-Dynasty Egyptian to thirteenth-century Islamic, being particularly strong in patterned, mould-blown vessels of the first six centuries AD.

The centre-piece of the collection, which, more than any other single item, attracted the public's attention and the envy of collectors, was a cage-cup, or *diatretum* (Fig 1), dating from about 300 AD. It is of colourless glass, and a remarkably well-preserved instance of these intricate Roman vessels, which were laboriously wheel-cut and polished *à jour* from thick, cast blanks by the Roman *diatretarii* (glass-cutters) as artistic and manipulative *tours de force*. There are two main groups. The first has figured decoration and in one instance network as well, and the second, network only. In both groups together, including all known fragments, there are thirty-seven examples, but so far only four complete or tolerably complete instances of the first group and seven of the second have been recorded, and only four other examples, although fragmentary, are fully restorable. Today, therefore, Roman cage-cups are rare and highly desirable, and, so far as is known, Constable-Maxwell's is the first to have reached a sale room. All the other tolerably complete examples have been safely immured, some for 150 years or more, in major European museums.

All the cups in the first group, with figured scenes, are entirely *sui generis*; and even in the second group, with network only, to which this cup belongs, we find that sufficient variations of detail occur – the presence or absence of convivial inscriptions, of an open-work overhanging flange above the network, of casing in one or more colours on a colourless base, and so on – to ensure that no example duplicates another and each is a unique masterpiece. Taking all this into account we would have been prepared for a high price. But this piece had other advantages: apart from some gaps in the network, some restoration on the rim and a few cracks in the body, it looked, and virtually was, a complete vessel. Its bowl-shaped profile, far wider than it was high, and its beautiful pale golden surface tints, deriving from mild lime-encrustation, covering advanced opaque-white flaking weathering, rendered it very pleasing to the eye. It is perhaps little wonder, therefore, that it fetched a price seven times higher than that of any glass vessel previously auctioned.

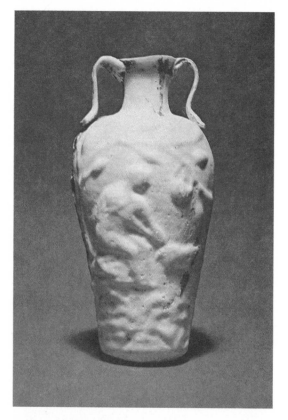

Fig 2
An opaque-white mould-blown 'Argonaut'
bottle, first century AD, height $3\frac{1}{4}$in (8.2cm)
London £12,000 ($24,600). 4.VI.79

Fig 3
A mould-blown cup inscribed *Rejoice since you are here*, first century AD,
height $2\frac{1}{8}$in (5.4cm)
London £12,000 ($24,600). 5.VI.79

Fig 4
A mould-blown cup inscribed *Made by Aristeas the Cypriote*, first half of the first century AD, height 2⅜in (6cm) London £75,000($153,750). 5.VI.79

But the collection was not devoid of other outstanding glasses. The price fetched by an immensely attractive first-century AD Romano-Syrian mould-blown cup of yellowish-green glass matched the previous record for a glass vessel (Fig 4). The cup is inscribed prominently on the side, *Made by Aristeas the Cypriote*. This maker's name, but without the designation 'Cypriote', was already recorded in a similar label on another vessel, a two-handled mould-blown cup found in the late nineteenth century at Albonese, Lombardy. To have a second piece by this maker is important enough; to find that it records his nationality is even more thrilling, for this is, in fact, the only first-century Romano-Syrian mould-blown glass on which the maker's place of origin is given. There can be no question but that the maker of this cup is the same man who signed the Albonese vessel. His two cups become the more interesting when we note that cups of the same exact shapes exist with labels bearing the signature of Ennion, the best-known and most prolific first-century Romano-Syrian glass-maker. So alike, indeed, are these Aristeas and Ennion vessels that the two men must have worked in close contact.

Besides this cup by Aristeas the collection contained three other first-century Romano-Syrian mould-blown vessels, but these bore convivial inscriptions only, without a maker's name. By far the most impressive was a cup with constricted and bulbous body inscribed in Greek, *Rejoice since you are here*; that is, as two people drinking together might now say, simply, 'Cheers' (Fig 3). The cup is of colourless glass, but appears blue because the weathering-film on the outside has been removed and what we see is the blue iridescence underlying the internal weathering-film. Several cups from this same mould have been recorded and there are others with the same inscription, but differing in profile and design. This example stands comparison with any of them both in preservation and tonal beauty.

Roughly equivalent in date are two other Romano-Syrian mould-blown vessels, each in a quite distinct style, which are of special interest because of the mythological content of their designs.

The first is a small opaque-white bottle blown in a two-part mould (Fig 2). Although insignificant in size, it bears two very carefully constructed scenes from the legend of the Golden Fleece and is thus far more deserving of attention than might at first appear. In the first scene Phryxus, having fled through the Hellespont to Colchis on a ram with a golden fleece sent to him by Zeus, sacrifices the ram to Zeus under a tree in the Grove of Ares. In the second scene we see Jason, sent by his uncle Pelias of Iolcos to fetch back the fleece, arriving at Colchis in the ship *Argo* rowed by the fifty Argonauts. The ship, mainsail reefed, approaches the shore with Jason at the bow and the helmsman, Tithys, at the stern. A fish and other marine life swim in the water below. At least three other such bottles, possibly more, all opaque-white and all seemingly from the same mould, are known, one with handles like this example, the other two with handles missing.

The second of these mythological vessels is far more distinguished in aspect, making an immediate impact on the beholder. It is an olive-green beaker, with a downward tapering profile and its design shows four figures advancing to the right, each in one of a row of columnar niches surmounted by pediments (Fig 5). The four figures are Heracles bearing a calf; Hymen, god of marriage, or a Season, with amphora and (?) a curved sickle; Hermes with ram's skull and caduceus; and Artemis, or a Season, bearing dead animals. The significance of this series of figures has so far eluded scholars, but this need not lessen the aesthetic and artistic interest of these glasses. In 1972 in volume XIV of the *Journal of Glass Studies* Mrs Weinberg discussed these glasses and their design in depth. She based her conclusions on the eight extant examples of the type then known to her, presenting good arguments in favour of the identifications cited above for the four figures. Other glasses of the same general type but with different figures exist, as Mrs Weinberg also showed.

Somewhat earlier than these first-century mould-blown vessels and formed by casting, manipulation and polishing rather than by blowing, is a fusiform or cigar-shaped hole-mouthed alabastron (Fig 6). Almost without doubt it once possessed a detachable hollow stopper that fitted into the mouth and allowed the liquid, or at least viscous, contents to be poured more slowly through its narrower opening. Complete examples with their stoppers exist in museums in Leiden, Boston and New York. The method of effecting the decoration, which is termed 'gold-band' because the alternating stripes include colourless ones with gold leaf embedded within them, has not yet been fully explained. It seems to have entailed moulding the stripes vertically first, releasing the partly-made vessel, and then twisting it freehand before a second moulding to attain its delightful serpentine effects. Many such vessels exist, but only a few of the finest are equal to this one in its excellent symmetry and its clarity of colouring.

Among the later glasses the two which most deserve attention are a late Sassanian or early Islamic oval dish decorated with bosses in high relief (Fig 8) and a very rare medieval European chalice and matching paten (Fig 7).

The oval dish, dark green with some iridescence, which is wheel-cut and polished

Fig 5
An olive-green mould-blown beaker, first
century AD, height 4⅞in (12.4cm)
London £35,000 ($71,750). 4.VI.79

from a thick, cast blank or a solid block, is decorated outside with ten circular and
four oval faceted bosses surrounding a large central boss, also faceted, on which the
vessel stands. This dish has, seemingly, no close parallel, though other types of oval
dish with cut decoration were common enough at this period. It belongs to a well-
recognised group of late sixth- to ninth-century Sassano-Islamic cut glasses with
raised decoration, of which the best known, and perhaps the finest, examples are a
number of colourless vessels in the Treasury of St Mark at Venice, notably two large,
shallow circular bowls which were probably used as hanging lamp-holders. These,
which were brought to Venice from Constantinople after the Frankish conquest in
1204, have traditionally been accounted Byzantine, and there are those who still
maintain this view; but the frequency of cast and cut vessels of these kinds in near
eastern countries and the apparent absence of any well-attested Byzantine parallels,
would appear to render incontrovertible their ascription to the Sassano-Islamic world
of the late sixth to the ninth centuries. This particular example falls, probably, fairly
late in the series, around the eighth or early ninth century.

Fig 6
A fusiform 'gold-band' alabastron, mid first
century BC – beginning of the first century AD,
height 4⅜in (11.1cm)
London £14,000 ($28,700). 4.VI.79

The medieval European chalice and matching paten are quite distinct in style and fabric from every other glass in the collection. The chalice has a cup-shaped bowl above a high, knopped stem and splayed foot; the paten is a plain, flat-bottomed saucer with low, outward curving sides, which fits neatly within the mouth of the chalice. Both are green, covered with a thick surface crust of mottled silvery-brown weathering, and the glass of both is so similar in colour and aspect that the two must come from the same batch. They were surely intended to be used together, almost certainly in the service of the church.

The real, basic difference between these two vessels and all the other Constable-Maxwell glasses is that, as their colouring and weathering-coats reveal, they are not soda glass but potash glass. As such they must have been made in Europe and not in the near east; for whereas soda glass was universal in the near east throughout antiquity and the middle ages, the use of potash instead of soda as alkali in glass-making was prevalent in many parts of Europe from the eleventh to the fifteenth century. Judging from the shape of the chalice, it is to the last half of that period that this particular pair of vessels most likely belongs. That they were made in Europe, however, does not necessarily imply that they were found there. They could very well have reached some part of the near east, taken there by a Christian pilgrim of high rank or by an ecclesiastical dignitary; no lesser person would have possessed such a pair in glass, since medieval chalices and patens were normally made of precious or base metal. Indeed, nothing comparable seems to have been recorded in glass from medieval times and the pair is, so far as our present knowledge extends, unique.

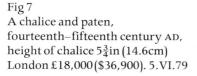

Fig 7
A chalice and paten,
fourteenth–fifteenth century AD,
height of chalice 5¾in (14.6cm)
London £18,000 ($36,900). 5.VI.79

Fig 8
A dark green oval dish, eighth–ninth century AD, length 6¼in (16cm)
London £11,000 ($22,550). 5.VI.79

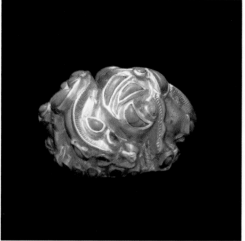

An Egyptian red jasper inlay, New Kingdom,
height 1½ in (3.7cm)
London £12,000 ($24,600). 10.VII.79
From the collection of His Highness
Prince Sadruddin Aga Khan

A Sarmatian gold finial inlaid with turquoise,
first century BC–first century AD,
height 1in (2.5cm)
New York $70,000 (£34,146). 14.XII.78

A Greek terracotta mask, fourth
century BC, height 8⅜in (21.3cm)
London £8,000 ($16,400). 10.VII.79
From the collection of the late
H. J. P. Bomford

An Egyptian limestone figure of a man, late fifth Dynasty, *circa* 2350–2290 BC,
height 31⅝in (80.3cm)
New York $280,000 (£136,585). 14.XII.78
From the collection of the Museum of Fine Arts, Boston

An Egyptian basalt head of a young woman, thirtieth Dynasty–early Ptolemaic period,
circa 380–250 BC, height 5in (12.7cm)
New York $150,000 (£73,171). 14.XII.78

An Egyptian bronze figure of Osiris enthroned, twenty-second Dynasty, probably period of Sheshonk I–Osorkon II, 946–861 BC, height 10¼in (26cm)
New York $57,000(£27,805). 14.XII.78
From the collection of Mr and Mrs S. N. Berman

A Roman bronze figure of Oikoumene, second half of the second century AD, height 8⅝in (22cm)
New York $46,000 (£22,439). 19.V.79
From the collection of Edwin L. Weisl Jr

This figure is a replica of the colossal marble personification of Oikoumene (Orbis Terrarum), which served as the lighthouse for the harbour known as Porto Raphti on the Attic coast. The beacon was formed from the large crown on her head and had to be lit each evening

A Hellenistic terracotta figure of a young woman, Myrina, second century BC,
height 12⅜in (31.5cm)
London £9,000 ($18,450). 10.VII.79
From the collection of the late H. J. P. Bomford

A Roman bronze bust of a lady, *circa* 20–30 AD, height 3⅜in (8.6cm)
New York $24,000(£11,707). 19.V.79
From the collection of Edwin L. Weisl Jr

This bust is probably of Antonia, daughter of Marc Antony, wife of Nero Claudius
Drusus, and mother of the Emperor Claudius

Chinese Ceramics and Works of Art

An archaic bronze animal-form standard, Western Chou Dynasty,
height 11⅜in (28.8cm)
New York $95,000 (£46,341). 5.V.79

A glazed pottery figure of a Bactrian camel, T'ang Dynasty, height 33½in (85cm)
London £58,000 ($118,900). 12.XII.78

A pair of glazed pottery figures of earth spirits, T'ang Dynasty, height 43¼in (110cm)
Monte Carlo FF 620,000 (£68,132:$139,670). 21.IV.79
From the Rudorff Collection

A white-glazed pottery ewer in the form of an Armenian wine seller, early T'ang
Dynasty, height 14in (35.5cm)
London £40,000 ($82,000). 12.XII.78

A glazed pottery ewer in the form of a lady, T'ang Dynasty, height 16in (40.7cm)
London £32,000 ($65,600). 3.IV.79

A glazed pottery tripod dish, T'ang Dynasty, diameter 11$\frac{1}{4}$in (28.5cm)
London £65,000 ($133,250). 12.XII.78

An Annamese polychrome storage jar, fifteenth century, height 22¼in (56.5cm)
London £28,000 ($57,400). 10.VII.79

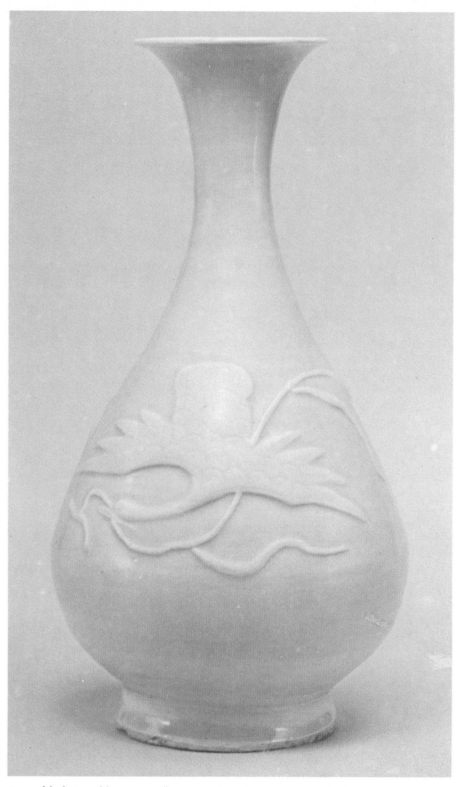

A moulded *ying-ch'ing* vase, Yüan Dynasty, height 11$\frac{1}{4}$in (28.5cm)
London £70,000 ($143,500). 10.VII.79

An underglaze-red decorated vase, Yüan Dynasty, height 9¼in (23.5cm)
London £48,000 ($98,400). 10.VII.79

A Ming blue and white stemcup, four character mark of Hsüan Tê, and of the period, height $4\frac{3}{8}$in (11.2cm)
Hong Kong HK $650,000(£61,905 : $126,905). 28.XI.78

A Ming blue and white ewer, period of Yung Lo, height 14¼in (36.2cm)
Hong Kong HK $2,000,000 (£190,476:$390,476). 28.XI.78

A Ch'ing blue and white altar vase, inscribed with a dedication by T'ang Ying, director of the Imperial Porcelain Manufacture, to a temple in Peking, dated 1740, period of Ch'ien Lung, height 25¼ in (64cm)
Hong Kong HK $270,000 (£25,714:$52,714). 22.V.79

Left
One of a pair of Ch'ing underglaze-blue and iron-red wine cups, six character marks
of Yung Chêng, and of the period, diameter $3\frac{1}{8}$in (8cm)
Hong Kong HK $92,000 (£8,762:$17,962). 22.V.79

Right
A Ch'ing *famille rose* waterpot and cover, seal mark of Ch'ien Lung, and of the period,
diameter $2\frac{7}{8}$in (7.3cm)
Hong Kong HK $45,000 (£4,286:$8,786). 22.V.79

A Ch'ing *famille rose* bowl, four character mark of K'ang Hsi in pink enamel, and of
the period, diameter $5\frac{5}{8}$in (14.3cm)
Hong Kong HK $360,000 (£34,286:$70,286). 22.V.79

Left and right A pair of Ch'ing aubergine-glazed dishes, six character marks of Yung Chêng, and of the period, diameter $4\frac{1}{2}$in (11.5cm)
Hong Kong HK $80,000 (£7,619 : $15,619). 28.XI.78

Centre A Ch'ing celadon vase, seal mark of Yung Chêng, and of the period, height $6\frac{1}{4}$in (15.9cm)
Hong Kong HK $75,000 (£7,143 : $14,643). 28.XI.78

A Ch'ing celadon vase, seal mark of Yung Chêng, and of the period,
height $5\frac{3}{4}$in (14.6cm)
Hong Kong HK $270,000 (£25,714:$52,714). 21.V.79

A Korean blue and white dragon jar, seventeenth – eighteenth century, height 20¾in (52.8cm)
London £40,000($82,000). 10.VII.79
From the collection of R. H. I. de la Mare

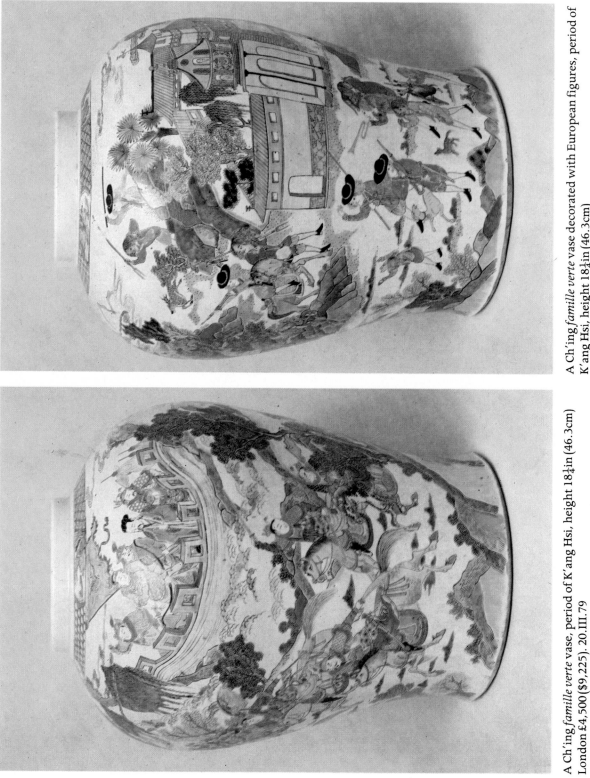

A Ch'ing famille verte vase, period of K'ang Hsi, height 18¼in (46.3cm)
London £4,500 ($9,225). 20.III.79

A Ch'ing famille verte vase decorated with European figures, period of
K'ang Hsi, height 18¼in (46.3cm)
London £9,500 ($19,475). 20.III.79

A painted leather wall hanging, eighteenth century, 7ft 7in by 5ft 8in (231.3cm by 172.7cm)
London £4,800 ($9,840). 15.VI.79

A jade bird finial, Six Dynasties,
height 2¼in (5.8cm)
New York $14,000 (£6,829). 4.XI.78

An archaic jade figure of a bear, Shang
Dynasty, height 1⅝in (4.2cm)
New York $35,000 (£17,073). 4.XI.78

These objects are from the collection of the late Rafi Y. Mottahedeh

A jade cosmetic box (*lien*), Sung Dynasty, height 4¾in (12cm)
New York $75,000 (£36,585). 10.II.79

A pure white jade covered tripod incense burner, period of Ch'ien Lung, height 10¼in (26cm)
New York $47,000(£22,927). 10.II.79

A Ming cinnabar lacquer dish, maker's mark of Chang Ch'êng, fourteenth century,
diameter 12¾in (32.4cm)
London £21,000 ($43,050). 12.XII.78
From the collection of Dr W. Balla

Opposite above
Two views of an engraved silver-gilt stemcup, T'ang Dynasty, height 3in (7.6cm)
London £62,000 ($127,100). 12.XII.78

Opposite below
An engraved silver-gilt bowl, late T'ang Dynasty, diameter 9½in (24.2cm)
London £39,000 ($79,950). 12.XII.78

A satin dragon robe (*ch'i fu*) brocaded with gold filé and silk, *circa* 1725
New York $3,000 (£1,463). 13.VI.79

Japanese Ceramics and Works of Art

A Kakiemon jar, late seventeenth century, height 7⅜in (18.8cm)
New York $35,000(£17,073). 28.IX.78

A Kakiemon vase, late seventeenth century, height $11\frac{3}{8}$in (29cm)
London £110,000 ($225,500). 29.III.79

An Ao-Kutani style bottle, late seventeenth century, height 10½ in (26.6cm)
London £34,000 ($69,700). 29.III.79
From the collection of R. H. I. de la Mare

A Haniwa model of a horse, Tumulus period, height 36in (91.5cm)
London £15,000($30,750). 29.III.79

A Shigaraki *mizusashi* (water-jar for tea ceremony), Muromachi–Momoyama
period, height 6¼in (16cm)
New York $27,000(£13,171). 23.V.79

Left
A gold and silver lacquer *inro* by Koma Koryu, signed, early nineteenth century
London £1,300 ($2,665). 8.XI.78

Right
A gold lacquer *inro*, probably by Kansai, early nineteenth century
Honolulu $4,600 (£2,244). 16.I.79

Above left
An iron *ojime* by Hitosuyanagi Tomonaga, signed, nineteenth century
Honolulu $2,600 (£1,268). 16.I.79

Above right
An iron *ojime*, nineteenth century
Honolulu $2,100 (£1,024). 16.I.79

An ivory group of two goats by Otoman, signed, Hakata, mid nineteenth century
London £6,000 ($12,300). 9.V.79

A gold and coloured lacquer *inro* by Yamada Jokasai, signed, nineteenth century
London £1,600 ($3,280). 29.III.79

A wood group of the San Sukumi by Sukeyuki, signed, nineteenth century
Honolulu $6,250 (£3,049). 16.I.79

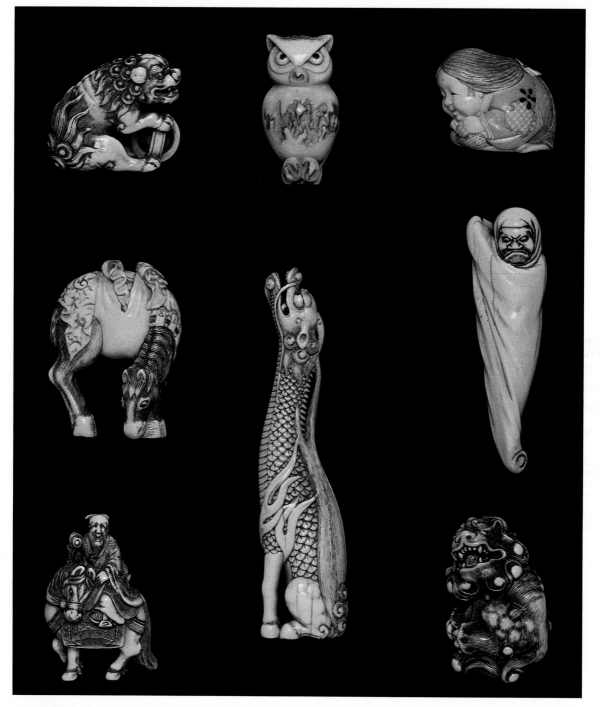

From left to right
An ivory study of a *shishi* by Okatomo, signed, Kyoto, eighteenth century, £2,600 ($5,330)
A staghorn study of an owl by Ozaki Kokusai, signed, Asakusa, nineteenth century, £10,500 ($21,525)
An ivory figure of Okame by Yasuaki (Homei), signed, Edo, twentieth century, £3,400 ($6,970)
An ivory study of a harnessed grazing horse, early nineteenth century, £1,400 ($2,870)
An ivory study of a *kirin* by Tomotada, signed, Kyoto, eighteenth century, £7,800 ($15,990)
An ivory figure of the ghost of Daruma, eighteenth century, £3,600 ($7,380)
An ivory figure of a sage by Yoshitomo, signed, Kyoto, late eighteenth century, £1,600 ($3,280)
An ivory study of a *shishi* by Risuke Garaku, signed, Osaka, eighteenth century, £1,700 ($3,485)

The *netsuke* on this page are from the collection of Mr and Mrs George A. Cohen and were sold in London on 7 March 1979

From left to right
An ivory figure of a girl by Isshin, signed, *circa* 1900, height 16½in (42cm)
£4,400 ($9,020)
An ivory group of a woman with a child by Ryumei, signed, Tokyo, *circa* 1900, height 19¾in (50cm)
£4,600 ($9,430)
An ivory group of three boys by Shumei, signed, Tokyo, *circa* 1900, height 16¾in (42.5cm)
£4,100 ($8,405)

The figures on this page are from the collection of the late G. S. Mottershead and were sold at Belgravia
on 8 March 1979

A metal box and cover by Jugykusai Ikkyu, the cover inset with a panel by
Sei To, signed, *circa* 1900, height 9⅝in (24.5cm)
Belgravia £8,200 ($16,810). 18.X.78

A lacquer *suzuribako* by Koma Kyuhaku, signed,
nineteenth century, height 8⅞in (22.5cm)
London £5,400 ($11,070). 29.III.79

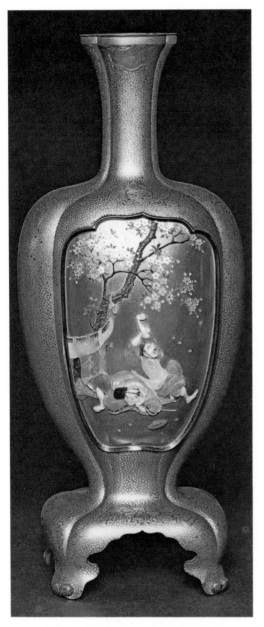

One of a pair of *shibayama* vases by Masayasu,
signed, *circa* 1900, height 9⅞in (25cm)
Belgravia £4,200 ($8,610). 28.VI.79

A lacquer box and cover by Ogawa Haritsu (Ritsuo), signed,
eighteenth century, height 11in (28cm)
London £4,200 ($8,610). 29.III.79

SUZUKI HARUNOBU
A young woman wanders down an 'engawa' holding a lantern into the night darkness
Chuban, unsigned, mid eighteenth century
New York $63,000 (£30,732). 24.V.79

TOSHUSAI SHARAKU
Ichikawa Omezo in the guise of a 'yakko' from the play 'Koinyobo Somewake Tazuna'
Oban, signed, late eighteenth century
New York $62,000 (£30,244). 24.V.79

A decorated iron *tsuba* by Hoshusei
Seiko, signed, diameter $3\frac{1}{8}$in (7.9cm)
London £3,400 ($6,970). 6.VI.79

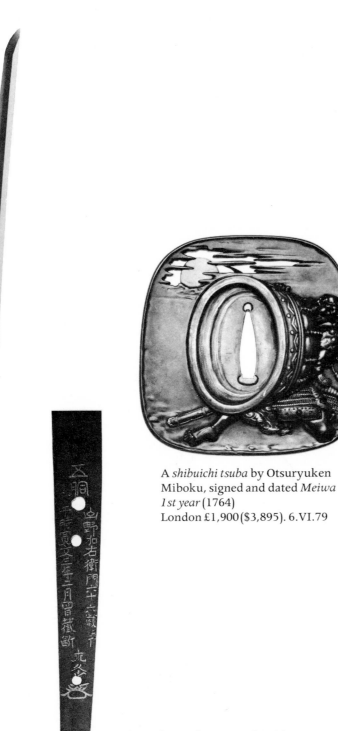

Detail

A *shibuichi tsuba* by Otsuryuken
Miboku, signed and dated *Meiwa
1st year* (1764)
London £1,900 ($3,895). 6.VI.79

A Shinto *katana* by Yasusada with
'Five Body' cutting attestation by
Nagahisa, Shirasaya, 1663, length
$29\frac{3}{4}$in (75.5cm)
New York $13,000 (£6,341). 25.I.79

A *sentoku tsuba* by a master of the
Shoami School, eighteenth century,
diameter $3\frac{5}{8}$in (9.2cm)
London £2,700 ($5,535). 6.VI.79

Arms and Armour

An American gold, diamond, silver and
enamel presentation sword, 1862,
length 40½in (103cm)
New York $34,000 (£16,585). 17.XI.78

This sword was presented by the citizens of
San Francisco to Major General Joseph
Hooker. Inscribed on the presentation
plaque is a list of Civil War battles in which
the General won particular distinction

One of a pair of d.b. 12-bore side-lock single-trigger ejector sporting guns by John Dickson & Son, serial numbers 7261/7262, length $45\frac{1}{2}$in (115.6cm)
Blair Castle £7,200 ($14,760). 9.VII.79

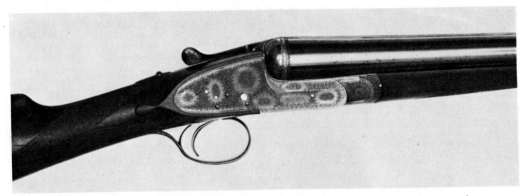

One of a pair of d.b. 12-bore side-lock single-trigger self-opening ejector sporting guns by Boss & Co, serial numbers 7867/7868, length $45\frac{1}{4}$in (115cm)
Blair Castle £11,000 ($22,550). 9.VII.79

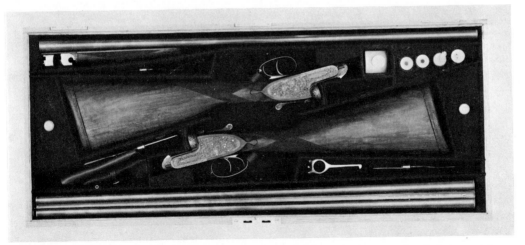

A pair of d.b. 12-bore side-lock self-opening ejector sporting guns by J. Purdey & Sons, serial numbers 27018/27019, length $45\frac{3}{8}$in (115.3cm)
London £11,000 ($22,550). 24.IV.79
From the collection of the late Sir Geoffrey Kitchen, TD

An engraved Mamluke arm guard with silver *koftgari* decoration, fifteenth–sixteenth century, length 18¼in (46.3cm)
London £5,200 ($10,660). 10.X.78

A pair of English silver-mounted flintlock holster pistols by I. Cosens, London, *circa* 1670, length 18¾in (47.6cm)
Blair Castle £7,000 ($14,350). 9.VII.79

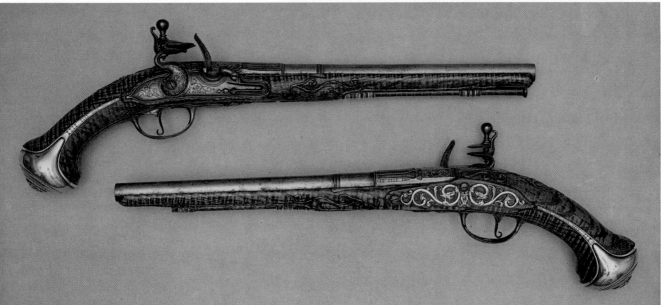

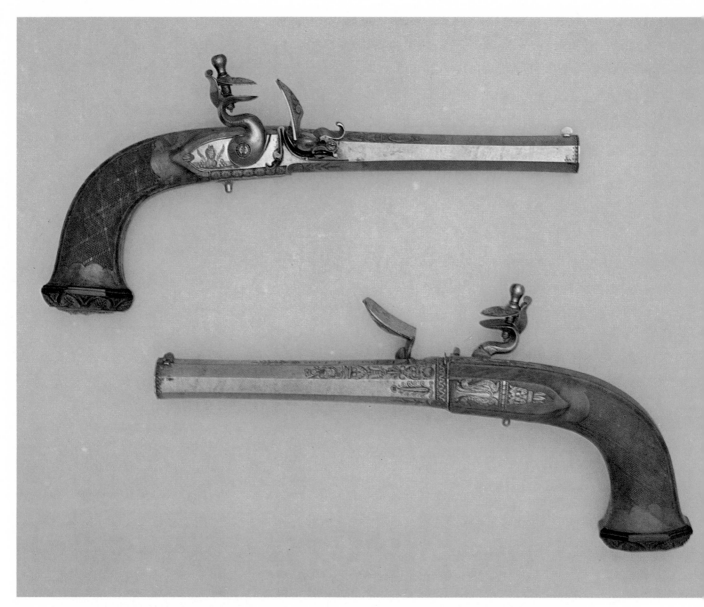

A pair of French flintlock travelling pistols by Jean Le Page, Paris, after 1815, length 11½in (29.2cm)
London £6,000 ($12,300). 24.IV.79

Works of Art

An ivory portrait medallion of a man by David Le Marchand, signed, *circa* 1700, height 8⅜in (21.3cm)
London £42,000 ($86,100). 14.XII.78

A Rhenish Romanesque gilt-bronze censer cover decorated with scenes from the Old Testament, inscribed *GODEFRIDVS FECIT TVRIBVLVN* (Godefroid made the censer), *circa* 1150,
height 4½in (11.5cm)
London £34,000 ($69,700). 12.VII.79

The four Old Testament scenes depicted are the Sacrifice of Abel, the Offering of Melchisedech, the Return of the spies from the Land of Canaan, and Moses and the brazen serpent. They can be identified by the inscription below each lunette

A German bronze vessel, inscribed *Hans Hachman à C* [Clèves] *anno XV ͨ 1* (1550),
height 6in (15.2cm)
London £12,500 ($25,625). 29.III.79
From the collection of Nils Tellander

A Nuremberg bronze aquamanile,
circa 1400, height 10in (25.4cm)
London £30,000 ($61,500). 29.III.79
From the collection of Major R.M.O.
de la Hey

A Limoges repoussé copper-gilt figure of Christ in Majesty, *circa* 1250, height 9⅜in (23.7cm)
New York $13,000(£6,341). 9.XII.78

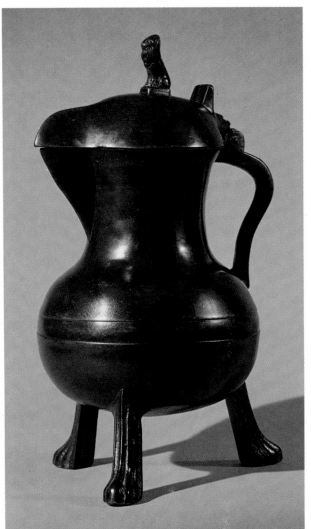

A Flemish brass pricket candlestick, mid fifteenth century, height 19¼in (48.9cm)
£10,000 ($20,500)

A North German or Netherlandish bronze covered pitcher, *circa* 1400, height 17½in (44.5cm)
£12,000 ($24,600)

The objects on this page are from the collection of Nils Tellander and were sold in London on 29 March 1979

A pair of English Gothic stained glass panels of the Virgin of the Annunciation and the Assumption of the Virgin, first half of the fifteenth century, height 31 in (78.8cm)
London £34,000 ($69,700). 29.III.79
From the collection of Dirk Laurens de Leur

These panels came from the chapel of Hampton Court, Leominster, Herefordshire. Other panels from the same chapel are now in Hereford Cathedral, the Victoria and Albert Museum, London, and the Museum of Fine Arts, Boston

The Trinity, the central relief of a Nottingham alabaster altar, the
other panels depicting Saints Stephen, Laurence, Erasmus and
Thomas, *circa* 1460–1500, height 20in (50.8cm)
London £57,000($116,850). 14.XII.78

A Rhenish Gothic polychrome walnut group of the Virgin and Child, *circa* 1370,
height 43in (109.2cm)
London £19,500 ($39,975). 14.XII.78

A Lorraine polychrome limestone group of the Virgin
and Child, *circa* 1380, height 34¾in (88.3cm)
London £13,000 ($26,650). 29.III.79

A Styrian polychrome wood figure of St Peter
attributed to the circle of the Master of Grosslobming,
circa 1415, height 22½in (57.2cm)
London £16,000 ($32,800). 29.III.79

A Rhenish limestone group of the Virgin and Child,
circa 1460, height 46½in (118.2cm)
London £17,500 ($35,875). 29.III.79

A Bavarian polychrome wood figure of
St John the Evangelist, probably from a
Crucifixion group, *circa* 1500,
height 46⅞in (119cm)
Munich DM38,000 (£9,620:$19,722). 17.V.79

A Netherlandish limewood relief of the Nativity, early sixteenth century, height 25⅝in (65cm)
Amsterdam Fl 45,000 (£10,465:$21,453). 7.XI.78

A Franconian gilt and polychrome wood triptych, early sixteenth century, height 80in (203.2cm)
New York $34,000 (£16,585). 8.XII.78
Formerly in the collection of the Museum of Art, Carnegie Institute

A gilt and polychrome wood group of the Virgin and Child enthroned, probably by a Flemish
sculptor working in Spain, *circa* 1530–40, height 65in (165cm)
El Quexigal Ptas1,900,000 (£13,971:$28,641). 26.V.79
From the collection of the Hohenlohe family

A pair of marble portrait busts of Laurence Sterne and Alexander Pope by Joseph Nollekens, late
eighteenth century, height 21in (53.3cm)
New York $35,000 (£17,073). 6.VI.79
From the collection of the late Benjamin Sonnenberg

A bronze bust of Paolo Giordano II Orsini, Duke of Bracciano, from a model by Gian Lorenzo Bernini,
Rome, seventeenth century, height 6½in (16.5cm)
London £8,500 ($17,425). 12.VII.79

A South German boxwood figure of a child attributed to Leonhard Kern, *circa* 1640, height 7in (17.7cm)
London £7,600 ($15,580). 14.XII.78

A Flemish alabaster allegorical carving attributed to Willem van den Broeck, *circa* 1560, length 12in (30.5cm)
London £11,000 ($22,550). 14.XII.78

A marble group of Cupid and Psyche by Giovanni Maria Benzoni, signed and dated *1851 Roma*, height 66½in (169cm)
Belgravia £17,000 ($34,850). 20.VI.79

A French bronze figure of a Taureg Camelier by Edouard Drouot, *circa* 1900, height 22in (55.8cm)
Belgravia £5,000 ($10,250). 29.XI.78

A pair of French bronze figures of a Japanese samurai and a young woman, *circa* 1875, height of each
24in and 25⅝in (61cm and 65cm)
Belgravia £2,800 ($5,740). 20.VI.79

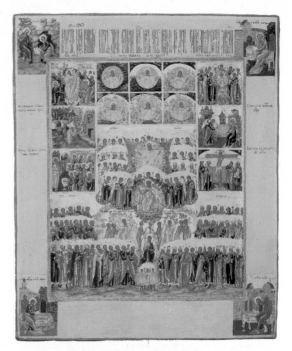

The 'Shestodnev', an icon with a scene for contemplation for each day of the week, nineteenth century, $12\frac{3}{8}$in by $10\frac{1}{4}$in (31.5cm by 26cm) Zurich SFr4,800 (£1,352:$2,772). 23.XI.78

A pair of royal sanctuary doors with scenes of the Annunciation and the four Evangelists, Moscow, *circa* 1600, $57\frac{1}{2}$in by $20\frac{1}{2}$in (146cm by 52cm) Zurich SFr70,000 (£19,718:$40,423). 23.XI.78

An icon of St John the Baptist and scenes from his life, repoussé silver-gilt and engraved oklad with maker's mark of F.T., Moscow, 1839, $13\frac{3}{4}$in by 12in (35cm by 30.5cm) Zurich SFr6,200 (£1,746:$3,580). 23.XI.78

An icon of the Archangel Michael by Michael Damaskinos, Crete, late sixteenth century, 39⅜in by 29½in (100cm by 75cm)
New York $56,000 (£27,317). 30.XI.78

Fig 1
A parcel-gilt and engraved beaker, inscribed *This beaker was ordered in 1560 by Gregory Lord of the Orcha for his dear friend Theodosia*, Moldavia, height 7⅞in (20cm)
Zurich SFr195,000(£54,930:$112,606). 22.XI.78

Russian silverware

M. M. Postnikova-Losseva

The large collection of Russian silverware, mainly from the seventeenth and eighteenth centuries, sold last November was the only one of its kind, unique in quality and scale. It provided a rare opportunity for Western collectors and specialists to study old Russian silver and to appreciate the extent of its varying styles.

The nucleus of the collection was acquired during the 1920s and '30s although the owner continued to add to it until his death in 1968. In 1932 a small edition of a catalogue with sixty illustrations was published in Paris. The collection largely comprised works by master silversmiths from Moscow, the most important cultural centre of the period, but there were also individual objects from cities throughout Russia. The works were primarily drinking vessels – *kovshi* (scoops), *bratini* (drinking bowls), *charki* (cups), beakers, *korchiki* (small scoops), tankards and goblets – embossed, engraved and decorated with enamel and niello, but there were also single examples of dinner and tea services from the latter part of the eighteenth century.

The silverware of ancient Russia is inherently calm with a stately rhythm of flowing line. The pieces have a rational form which always corresponds to their use, a sense of harmony between form and decoration and an absence of anything disturbing to the eye. The art of the silversmith grew from basic folk craft. The shape of traditional wooden ladles which had been established over the centuries, solid, functional and skilfully decorated, evolved into that of the silver *kovshi*. The wooden *kovshi* originated in the forests of the north, an area abundant in rivers and lakes and teeming with waterfowl, where wooden canoes resembled floating birds. Fragments of carved birds' heads and wooden *kovshi*, dating from as early as 2000 BC, have been discovered by an archaeological expedition in the Urals organised by the Moscow Historical Museum.

The first reference to gold and silver *kovshi* and the first representation of them, in manuscript illustrations, date from the fourteenth century. This new form of precious vessel – a boat-like, almost round scoop with raised sides – originated in Novgorod. Later, in the sixteenth century, a more refined type of *kovsh* was developed in Moscow – oval, shallower, light and elegant. It was used for drinking mead, an ancient drink known from documents to have been brewed in Russia since the tenth century. Made from honey boiled with water and various berries, it was then spiced with cinnamon and nutmeg. At court banquets of the seventeenth century these vessels were treated with aesthetic sensitivity, only the red mead was poured into

Fig 2
A parcel-gilt *bratina* inscribed *Bratina of an honest man, drink from it to your health*, early seventeenth century, height 4⅛in (10.5cm)
Zurich SFr11,000(£3,099:$6,352). 22.XI.78

Fig 4
A silver-gilt *bratina*, inscribed *Alexei Petrovich, Great Sovereign, Grand Prince and Noble Tzarevich of all Great, Little and White Russia*, Moscow, probably 1693, height 1⅞in (4.8cm)
Zurich SFr6,500(£1,831:$3,754). 22.XI.78

Now in the Historical Museum, Moscow

Fig 3
A silver-gilt *kovsh* with a cast and chased silver imperial eagle, and the cypher of Catherine II, late eighteenth century, length 12⅝in (32cm)
Zurich SFr55,000(£15,493:$31,761). 22.XI.78

Fig 5
A silver-gilt *kovsh*, late seventeenth century, length 11¾in (30cm)
Zurich SFr28,000(£7,887:$16,168). 22.XI.78

Presented by Peter I to Michael Xenophontov, customs official responsible for the administration of government liquor tax in Solikamsk, 1690

Fig 6
A silver-gilt *kovsh* engraved with a portrait of Peter II, mid eighteenth century, length 10in (25.5cm)
Zurich SFr40,000(£11,268:$23,099). 22.XI.78

Fig 7
A parcel-gilt and engraved *kovsh*, late seventeenth century, length 12¾in (32.5cm)
Zurich SFr45,000 (£12,676:$25,986). 22.XI.78

golden *kovshi*, while the white was poured into silver ones. The Tzar's health was then toasted around the table, a custom which survived among the Don Cossacks well into the eighteenth century.

Before the introduction of medals in Russia, various services were rewarded by gifts of richly-woven clothes, horses, money or silverware. At first the silver vessels were taken from the Tzar's kitchens but in the second half of the seventeenth century when *kovshi* acquired special significance as a token of imperial favour they began to be made to a particular design. This included an obligatory representation of the two-headed eagle on the bottom and a solemn inscription setting out the Tzar's titles, the recipient's name and a reference to his services.

The variety of services rewarded was well illustrated by the collection and included governing the towns of Arzamas and Dorogobuzh, military service, 'wounds and injuries', collecting customs duty. A beautiful *kovsh* bearing a portrait of the young Peter I after Godfrey Kneller, was awarded for developing trade with China, and a number of *kovshi* were presented to the Don Cossacks 'for loyal service', among them a particularly rare example engraved with a portrait of the youthful Peter II (Fig 6). However, the great majority of silver *kovshi* were awarded for the administration of taxes levied on wine, as these sums represented a significant contribution to the state income (Fig 5).

Gradually, as the *kovsh* was used less for drinking and more for awards, its shape began to change becoming increasingly elaborate and losing its resemblance to the silhouette of a floating bird. The handle lost its gentle curve and its suggestion of a bird's head, the sharp raised tip (the duck's tail) was replaced by decorations in the form of a two-headed eagle or a flower bud and, because of the two-headed eagle engraved on it, the base ceased to be flat (cf. Figs 3 and 7). The long inscriptions were set out around the sides of the vessels in circles or between parallel lines and became an important decorative feature as well as adding to the significance of the *kovsh* as an historical document.

Another national form of ancient Russian vessel was the *bratina*. Like the *kovsh* it also has its roots in folk art; its almost circular shape, narrowed at the top and bottom, is reminiscent of ancient ceramic vessels. It was customary to pass *bratini* around the table for toasts at banquets, in the same way as *kovshi*. Russian drinks, mainly mead, were drunk from them, while wine was handed round in goblets. In addition, on days of remembrance, *bratini*, filled with a special mixture of mead and water, were placed on tombs.

Russian silversmiths knew how to bring out the natural beauty of their metal by means of prolonged hammering. A large part of the surface of the *bratina* was left free of ornament and what decoration there was served to emphasise the form, as can be seen in the early seventeenth-century example in this collection (Fig 2). From a band of engraved arabesques a delicate pattern falls freely over the side of the vessel accentuating its shape. The small child's *bratina* which once belonged to Peter I's son, the Tzarevich Alexei Petrovich, shows a simplified version of this design (Fig 4). It was probably made in 1693 when the Tzarevich was three years old.

In the seventeenth century a number of drinking-bowls similar in form to *bratini* were made in Hamburg exclusively for the Russian market. Customers' names are engraved on many of the surviving examples which are somewhat heavier and lack the magical, flowing lines of the original shape and its unity of decoration and form.

Korchiki and *charki* appeared with the introduction of strong liquors, such as vodka, in the seventeenth century. Both were well represented in the collection and are remarkable for the wealth of fantasy shown by the silversmiths, who decorated them inside and out with repoussé and embossed images and designs, and engraved inscriptions citing the owners' names and appropriate proverbs (Figs 9 and 10). Whereas *charki* are round, *korchiki* are oval with a handle and prow, and are raised on a flared base (Fig 8). Those made in Novgorod, some of which are on legs in the forms of lions or gryphons, are especially beautiful and elegant. Many of them have a handle cast in the form of a vase of flowers or the more intricate design of Samson tearing apart a lion's jaws, while the finial is shaped as a helmeted head or flower bud.

Fig 8
A silver-gilt *korchik*, inscribed *True love is
like a golden vase which never breaks*,
Novgorod, late seventeenth century,
height 2¾in (7.2cm)
Zurich SFr5,000 (£1,408:$2,887). 22.XI.78

Fig 9
A repoussé silver-gilt *charka*, inscribed
*Charka of an honest man, drink from it
to your health, praising God*, the interior
depicting Jonah and the whale,
seventeenth century, height 1¾in (4.6cm)
Zurich SFr2,500 (£704:$1,443). 22.XI.78

Fig 10
A repoussé silver-gilt *charka*, the interior
depicting Jonah and the whale,
seventeenth century, height 1⅝in (4cm)
Zurich SFr3,500 (£986:$2,021). 22.XI.78

Fig 11
Part of a parcel-gilt and niello service by Semyon Petrov Kuzov, Moscow, 1798–99, made for Count Nikolai Sherimetiev

A soup tureen and cover, SFr102,000 (£28,732:$58,900)
Eight of fourteen silver-gilt dessert plates, SFr42,000 (£11,831:$24,254)
A pair of sauce tureens without covers, SFr45,000 (£12,676:$25,986)

The objects on this page were sold in Zurich on 22 November 1978

Fig 12
A silver-gilt and niello holy-water bowl
by Matvey Ageev silversmith of the
Kremlin workshops, dated *1692*, Moscow,
height 5$\frac{7}{8}$in (15cm)
Zurich SFr25,000(£7,042:$14,436). 22.XI.78

Now in the Historical Museum, Moscow

In no other country has niello been used for as long a period and in such a variety of ways. The collection included many distinctive early examples made in Moscow and other centres at the end of the seventeenth century. These are characterised by boldly engraved and gilded decoration on a densely covered background of tiny nielloed herbs and flowers. An important work of this period was the silver-gilt holy-water bowl with a gilt floral design on a nielloed background (Fig 12). An inscription states that it was commissioned by Archimandrite Varfolomey at his own expense, on 21 November 1692, and was given by him to the Trinity Monastery at Pereslavl. The bowl was made by Matvey Ageev, a silversmith employed in the workshops of the Moscow Kremlin. The Armoury Museum of the Kremlin has another of his works, which is dated 1695.

During the eighteenth and nineteenth centuries Moscow, Veliky Ustyug, Vologda and Tobolsk were the most important centres of niello work and the collection included a wide range of objects from these cities. One of the most beautiful works made in Moscow at the end of the eighteenth century was by Semyon Petrov Kuzov (Fig 11). It is a silver-gilt soup tureen, striking for its well-proportioned beauty of form and decorated with niello images of antique scenes on an engraved background of fish-scaling. The Sherimetiev coat-of-arms is shown in an oval medallion indicating the family for whom this tureen and the accompanying service were made. The lid is crowned by a flower finial while at either end of the oval tureen there are lions' heads with rings in their mouths. This piece surpasses all known works by Kuzov, many of which are owned by museums in Moscow, Leningrad and Kaluga.

The oldest and most unusual piece in the collection was a tall parcel-gilt beaker engraved with a design of intertwining snakes (Fig 1). The form of the beaker and the design and style of the inscription distinguish it from purely Russian works and indicate that it was produced in a different cultural environment. The arrangement of the inscriptions on ribbons and the style of lettering suggest that the beaker was made in Moldavia. Similar beakers are very rare, in fact only four others are known, those in the Margineli and Tisman monasteries, in the Russian Museum, Leningrad and in the Armoury Museum of the Kremlin, Moscow.

A silver-gilt and shaded enamel *kovsh*, maker's
mark of Kuzma Konov, Moscow, 1899–1908,
length 5½in (14cm)
Zurich SFr17,000(£4,789:$9,817). 23.XI.78

A silver-gilt and shaded enamel beaker, maker's
mark of Maria Semyenova, Moscow, late
nineteenth century, height 7⅞in (20cm)
Zurich SFr18,000(£5,070:$10,394). 23.XI.78

A silver-gilt and *champlevé* enamel casket, maker's mark of
Pavel Ovchinnikov, Moscow, 1877, length 7½in (19cm)
New York $8,500(£4,146). 30.XI.78

A Fabergé gold, enamel and diamond imperial presentation box inset with a miniature of Nicholas II, workmaster Mikhail Perchin, St Petersburg, late nineteenth century, width 3¼in (8.3cm)
New York $65,000 (£31,707). 28.VI.79
From the collection of Dr Sidney Levine

The box is enamelled with the colours of the royal house of Denmark and was a gift from Nicholas II to his mother, Maria Feodorovna, who was born a Princess of Denmark

A Fabergé nephrite dish, the handles set with the monograms of Nicholas II and Alexandra
Feodorovna, workmasters Mikhail Perchin and Henrik Wigström, St Petersburg, *circa* 1900,
width 23⅜in (59.5cm)
Zurich SFr130,000 (£36,620:$75,070). 17.V.79

A Fabergé hardstone figure of the boy who was *dvornik* (houseboy or yardman) at Fabergé's St Petersburg premises, St Petersburg, 1899–1908, height 4⅞ in (12.5cm)
SFr110,000 (£30,986 : $63,521)

A Fabergé hardstone figure of a *hohol* (Ukranian peasant), St Petersburg, *circa* 1900, height 5¼ in (13.2cm)
SFr75,000 (£21,127 : $43,310)

These figures are from the collection of the John R. Cowdy family and were sold in Zurich on 23 November 1978

An English enamel plaque, possibly London, *circa* 1760, height 5⅞in (15cm)
New York $2,500(£1,220). 1.VI.79

A jewelled gold snuff box, maker's mark of François Marteau, Paris, 1743, width 3in (7.6cm)
Zurich SFr105,000(£29,577:$60,634). 23.XI.78

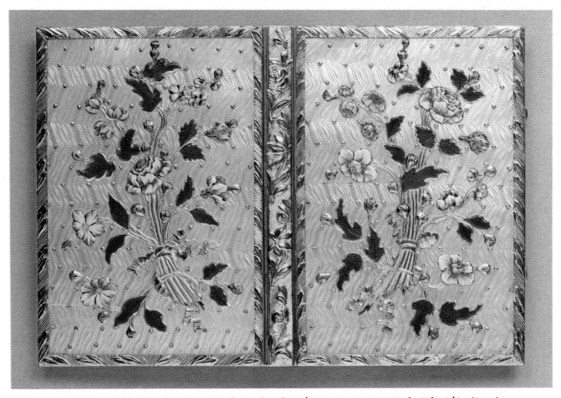

A two-colour gold, enamel and mother-of-pearl *aide-mémoire*, Paris, 1748, height 3½in (9cm)
London £17,000($34, 850). 18.VI.79

A two-colour gold and enamel snuff box, maker's mark of Pierre-Nicolas Queneulle de Romesnil,
Paris, 1763, width 2¾in (7.1cm)
London £40,000 ($82,000). 18.VI.79

A gold and enamel snuff box attributed to Frantz Bergs, probably Swedish, *circa* 1755,
width 3⅛in (8cm)
London £33,000 ($67,650). 18.VI.79

A gold-mounted shell snuff box, maker's mark of Pierre-François Mathis de Beaulieu, Paris, 1774, width 3½in (9cm)
London £7,000 ($14,350). 18.VI.79
From the collection of His Highness Prince Sadruddin Aga Khan

An English gold snuff box, *circa* 1740, length 3¼in (8.2cm)
Zurich SFr 68,000 (£19,155:$39,268). 23.XI.78

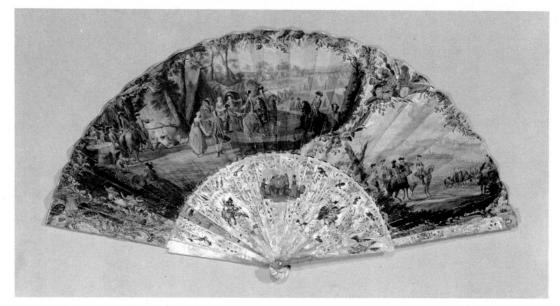

A paper fan decorated with scenes of military parades in the style of Adam Frans van der Meulen, with mother-of-pearl sticks, 1700–1750, width 11⅜in (29cm)
Amsterdam Fl 4,600 (£1,070:$2,194). 4.XII.78

A paper fan decorated with a scene depicting Bacchus and Ariadne, with mother-of-pearl sticks, eighteenth century, width 11⅜in (29cm)
Amsterdam Fl 3,100 (£721:$1,478). 4.XII.78

A carved ivory table centre-piece of the triumph of Bacchus, probably French, *circa* 1850–75,
length 48¾in (124cm)
Belgravia £28,000 ($57,400). 8.III.79
From the collection of the late G. S. Mottershead

P. or L. CROSSE
The Earl of Ossory, KG, signed with
monogram, *circa* 1660, $2\frac{1}{4}$in (5.8cm)
London £5,800 ($11,890). 11.XII.78

NICHOLAS DIXON
Sir Willoughby Aston, signed with
monogram, *circa* 1690, $2\frac{7}{8}$in (7.4cm)
London £2,000 ($4,100). 26.III.79

SCHOOL OF LEVINA TEERLINC
Lady Katherine Graye (*sic*),
circa 1550, $1\frac{3}{8}$in (3.4cm)
London £8,500 ($17,425).
25.VI.79

Lady Katherine was the sister of
Lady Jane Grey

FRANCISZEK SMIADECKI
Called Jan de Witt, on copper,
circa 1660, $2\frac{3}{8}$in (6cm)
London £2,200 ($4,510).
25.VI.79

P. or L. CROSSE
Lady Diana Graye (*sic*), signed
with monogram, *circa* 1700,
$2\frac{3}{4}$in (7cm)
London £6,000 ($12,300). 25.VI.79

RICHARD COSWAY
Master Bunbury, signed on the reverse
and dated *1802*, 3⅜in (8.5cm)
London £18,000 ($36,900). 25.VI.79

ANDREW PLIMER
Two children, *circa* 1800, 3in (7.7cm)
London £3,000 ($6,150). 25.VI.79

SIMON JACQUES ROCHARD
The Duke of Wellington, KG, signed and dated
1815, 3¼in (8.3cm)
London £6,200 ($12,710). 11.XII.78

RICHARD COSWAY
A young man, signed on the reverse and dated
1799, 3⅛in (8cm)
London £4,000 ($8,200). 11.XII.78

HEINRICH FRIEDRICH FÜGER
Friederike Charlotte and Juliane Wilhelmine Bause,
on ivory, *circa* 1772, 3¼in (8.4cm)
Zurich SFr90,000 (£25,352:$51,972). 17.V.79

DMITRI EVREINOV
Empress Catherine II seated at a
writing table before a marble bust of
Peter the Great, enamel, *circa* 1800,
4¼in (10.7cm)
Zurich SFr15,500 (£4,366:$8,951).
24.XI.78

JEAN-BAPTISTE ISABEY
Four small children, signed, *circa* 1810, $2\frac{3}{4}$in (7cm)
London £5,200 ($10,660). 26.III.79

LOUIS LIE PERIN-SALBREUX
A young child, signed, *circa* 1795, $2\frac{5}{8}$in (6.6cm)
Zurich SFr12,500 (£3,521:$7,218). 17.V.79

ADOLF THEER
A young girl, *circa* 1840, $3\frac{1}{8}$in (8cm)
Zurich SFr5,400 (£1,521:$3,118). 17.V.79

JEAN-BAPTISTE AUGUSTIN
A young girl, signed and dated *1815*, $3\frac{1}{2}$in (9cm)
Zurich SFr10,000 (£2,817:$5,775). 24.XI.78

GERMAN SCHOOL
A lady and gentleman taking tea, on vellum, *circa* 1750, $4\frac{5}{8}$in (11.7cm) London £3,000 ($6,150). 11.XII.78

JOHANN ANTON PETERS
A lady, on vellum, signed and dated *1754*, $2\frac{7}{8}$in (7.4cm)
Zurich SFr7,000 (£1,972:$4,043). 17.V.79

MORITZ MICHAEL DAFFINGER
A young lady, signed, *circa* 1835, $4\frac{1}{2}$in (11.5cm)
Zurich SFr9,500 (£2,676:$5,486). 24.XI.78

Silver and Pewter

One of a pair of Queen Anne silver-gilt salvers, maker's mark of Simon Pantin, London, 1713, diameter 15in (38cm)
London £28,000 ($57,400). 30.XI.78
From the collection of Gerald Hochschild

The arms are those of Fetherstone of Blackesware, for Sir Henry Fetherstone, 2nd Bt, who succeeded his father on 23 October 1711. When he died on 17 October 1746 the baronetcy became extinct

A George III soup tureen with cover and stand and a pair of George III sauce tureens with covers and stands, maker's marks of Paul Storr, London, 1807–1808, width of soup tureen 21in (53.4cm)
London £27,000 ($55,350). 30.XI.78

One of a pair of George III wine coolers, maker's mark of William Pitts, London, 1801, height $9\frac{1}{4}$in (23.5cm)
London £8,500 ($17,425). 26.IV.79

A pair of Queen Anne silver-gilt jugs, maker's mark of John Backe, London, 1705, height 11¼in (28.6cm)
London £20,000($41,000). 30.XI.78
From the collection of Gerald Hochschild

The arms are those of Bertie with Wynn in pretence for Robert, 4th Earl of Lindsey, and his wife Mary, daughter of Sir Richard Wynn, Bt, whom he married in 1678. He succeeded his father in 1701

An American presentation punch bowl, maker's mark of Hugh Wishart, New York, *circa* 1799, diameter 13½in (34.3cm)
New York $105,000 (£51,220). 20.VI.79

The arms and crest are those of Captain William D. Seton, to whom the bowl was presented in 1799 by the president and directors of the New York Insurance Company in recognition of his defence of his ship against a French attack of superior force in the Bay of Bengal

A pair of George II double-lipped sauce boats and ladles, maker's marks of Lewis Herne
and Francis Butty, London, 1757, width of sauce boats 7⅛in (18cm)
Zurich SFr 36,000 (£10,141:$20,789). 22.XI.78

A pair of German silver-gilt toilet boxes, maker's mark of Gottlieb Satzger, Augsburg,
1753–55, width 10in (25.3cm)
Zurich SFr 90,000 (£25,352:$51,972). 22.XI.78

A William and Mary livery badge, inscribed *A la volonté de Dieu*, maker's mark of Robert Cooper, London, 1693, width 7¾in (19.7cm)
London £1,800($3,690). 19.VII.79

The crest is that of Strickland of Boynton, Co. Yorks. The Strickland family were credited with the introduction of the domestic turkey into England, and in arms granted in 1560 the vert is 'a turkey cock in his pride proper'

A William and Mary Monteith bowl, London, 1689, diameter 10¼in (26cm)
London £13,000($26,650). 26.IV.79

A German parcel-gilt tankard engraved with scenes from the Old Testament, *circa* 1630, height 13½in (34.3cm)
New York $16,000(£7,805). 12.X.78

A pair of Dutch sugar castors, maker's mark
of Reynier de Haan, The Hague, 1772,
height $9\frac{1}{2}$in (24cm)
Amsterdam Fl 22,000 (£5,116:$10,488). 7.XI.78

One of a set of four Louis XV salts, maker's mark of
J. B. F. Chèret, Paris, 1762, height $3\frac{3}{4}$in (9.5cm)
Zurich SFr 38,000 (£10,704:$21,944). 16.V.79

A Swiss soup tureen and cover, maker's mark of Ernst Wilhelm Hundeshagen, Fribourg,
circa 1750, width $11\frac{3}{8}$in (29cm)
Zurich SFr 22,000 (£6,197:$12,704). 16.V.79

A Japanese Imari bowl and
cover with Louis XV silver-
gilt mounts, Paris, 1737,
width 7½in (19cm)
Zurich SFr 45,000
(£12,676:$25,986). 16.V.79

One of a pair of Louis XV meat dishes, maker's mark of Alexis Loir, Paris, 1744, width 14⅜in (36.7cm)
Zurich SFr 70,000 (£19,718:$40,423). 16.V.79

ORIENTAL.

Silver Dessert Stand, with Ostrich
under Palm Tree, 20 in. high ... £47 0 0

Fig 1
An engraving of the 'Oriental pattern' dessert
stand from the illustrated catalogue of The
Goldsmiths' Alliance Ltd, 38th edition. An
identical stand, maker's mark of Alexander
Macrae, London, 1870, was sold at Belgravia on
6 November 1975 for £380

Fig 2
A candelabrum probably made by the firm of Benjamin Smith
of Lincoln's Inn Fields, 1830, being wheeled by Edward Sinper
of the Pall Mall Safe Deposit, to a refinery for melting down in
December 1954

Attitudes to Victorian silver in the melting pot

John Culme

The mid nineteenth-century art historian, Matthew Digby Wyatt, once launched into a preposterous survey of three centuries of English silver. Conceding that what was best in workmanship 'may be traced to the times of Henry VIII, Elizabeth, the two Charleses, and Queen Anne', he finished by observing that the styles in plate of the latter were succeeded by 'a poor imitation of Louis Quinze work, degenerating at last through the thin and meagre style of the Adamses, into the pretentious and feeble handling which distinguished almost all that issued from the ateliers of the great court goldsmiths Rundell and Bridge'. His sweeping dismissal of late eighteenth- and early nineteenth-century silver was as much an emotional rejection of the new mass-production techniques as it was the result of his artistic judgement. In spite of the efforts of Octavius Morgan and William Chaffers in the 1850s and '60s to unravel the English hallmarking system, thereby encouraging a more rational approach to the subject, there are still a surprising number of people who share Wyatt's views.

During the last thirty years, however, this once fashionable trend to condemn most nineteenth-century work has gradually given way to more tolerant consideration. N. M. Penzer's monograph, *Paul Storr, last of the goldsmiths*, 1954, a gravely unbalanced account of its subject's career, was nonetheless a step towards an appreciation of late Georgian and early Victorian silver at a time when many large display items appearing on the market were in danger of being sent off to the refiners (Fig 2). One is tempted to ask what has become of the 10,000 ounce fountain made and shipped to Egypt in 1845 by the firm of Benjamin Smith, or the equally extraordinary six-foot high candelabrum of silver and damascened iron made by Antoine Vechte at Hunt & Roskell to house the celebrated Poniatowski gems. Indeed, as late as 1967 a massive charger made in 1847 at Edward Barnard & Sons for presentation by the Liverpool Anti-Monopoly Association failed to find a buyer at Sotheby's and was subsequently melted down. Later research revealed that the figure of Britannia at its centre was in fact a portrait of Queen Victoria and the piece had been one of the chief exhibits of Joseph Mayer, the Liverpool retail silversmith, at the Great Exhibition of 1851.

In England the growing number of collectors of Victorian silver owe much to the pioneer work of Patricia Wardle in her book, *Victorian Silver and Silver-plate*, 1963, and of Shirley Bury in her splendid series of three articles, 'The lengthening shadow of Rundells' for *The Connoisseur* in 1966. Three years after Mrs Bury's articles were

Fig 3
A neo-rococo wine cooler, maker's mark of John
S. Hunt of Hunt & Roskell, London, 1844, height
$10\frac{1}{2}$in (26.6cm)
New York $4,750(£2,317). 12.XII.78

Fig 4
A four-piece tea and coffee set, maker's mark of George Angell, London, 1852
Belgravia £2,300 ($4,715). 29.III.79

Fig 5
A mustard pot, maker's mark of
James Barclay Hennell,
London, 1880, length 3½in (9cm)
Belgravia £180($369). 12.X.78

published, Sotheby's instituted sales devoted entirely to silver 'from the reigns of William IV and Queen Victoria', the first of which took place on 17 March 1969. Already apprehensive, the organisers were further alarmed on the morning to find only a handful of people in the room. The sale went well, however, and confirmed long-held opinions that Victorian silver, and even electroplate, were already accepted among regular buyers of silver. During the ten years since that first sale there has been a general reappraisal of Victoriana, reinforced in saleroom circles by the opening of Sotheby's Belgravia in 1971.

This season has seen the appearance of several remarkable items including the neo-rococo wine cooler made at Hunt & Roskell (Fig 3), the design of which doubtless owes its inspiration to a group of mid eighteenth-century engravings in the only surviving source book belonging to their predecessors, Storr & Mortimer.[1] The Angells, best known today for the 1851 Aesop's Fables tea and coffee service sold at Belgravia in 1973, were again represented by a set of typically novel design (Fig 4).

Victorian silver, and related wares such as jewellery and objects of vertu, still offer much scope to collectors of both a serious and a whimsical turn of mind. Although gaps exist in the available documentary material, such as the disappearance of the ledgers of Rundell, Bridge & Rundell, Storr & Mortimer and Hunt & Roskell, and those of the nineteenth century for Garrards, a vast amount remains largely untapped. Special orders, exhibition pieces and presentation or racing plate were often reported in the press; and at Christmas time, especially in the 1880s and '90s, ladies' periodicals gave illustrated information on all the latest novelties. The catalogues of the retail and manufacturing silversmiths of some hundred years ago, A. B. Savory & Sons, later The Goldsmiths' Alliance Ltd, or Elkington & Co to name but two, abound in illustrations of everything from tea sets to centre-pieces which now regularly appear at sales (Fig 1). Matthew Digby Wyatt and his like-minded contemporaries may not have been amused by unwieldy candelabra or pig-shaped, not to mention pig-headed, mustard pots (Fig 5), but today their popularity is firmly re-established.

[1] This volume is now in the Silver and Vertu Department, Sotheby's Belgravia. It largely comprises European engravings of vases and cups dating from the sixteenth to eighteenth centuries, and the penultimate page is inscribed *No 201 Storr & Mortimer 13 New Bond St*

Part of a table suite, maker's mark of A. Aucoc, Paris, late nineteenth century, width
of soup tureen 24in (61cm)
Belgravia £5,500 ($11,275). 14.XII.78

Opposite
The centre-piece of a parcel-gilt table garniture, maker's mark of Frederick Elkington
of Elkington & Co, Birmingham, 1881, width 14¾in (37.5cm)
New York $25,000 (£12,195). 12.XII.78

A Grand Prix du Yacht Club de France trophy comprising a soup tureen with cover and stand, maker's mark of Robert Linzeler, Paris, *circa* 1905, width of soup tureen 20¼in (51.5cm)
Belgravia £8,500 ($17,425). 14.XII.78

This trophy is said to have been won by Kaiser Wilhelm II for the European Yacht championship. In 1913 he returned it to the Yacht Club de France for a new competition, when it was won by F. Milburn of Newcastle-on-Tyne and Sir Thomas Lipton at the International Regatta at Le Havre

Left
An American silver-gilt and ivory covered cup by Joseph Fischer, New York, 1918,
height 21½in (54.6cm)
New York $5,500(£2,683). 13.X.78

Right
An American silver-gilt and ivory tankard by Joseph Fischer, New York, *circa* 1905,
height 21¾in (55.3cm)
New York $10,500(£5,122). 13.X.78

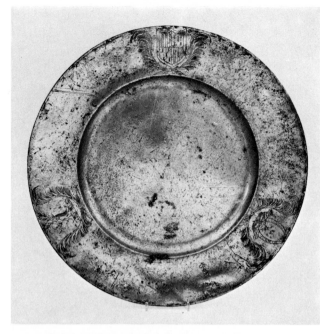

An English broad-rimmed charger, *circa* 1660,
diameter 24¾in (62.9cm)
London £1,050 ($2,153). 15.III.79

Two German guild cups and covers, eighteenth
century, height of each 22⅝in (57.5cm), 25in (63.5cm)
London £650 ($1,333); £620 ($1,271). 11.VI.79

A Dutch 'Rembrandtkan' flagon, *circa* 1700,
height 8⅞in (22.5cm)
London £1,150 ($2,358). 23.XI.78

An American quart tankard, maker's mark of William Will,
Philadelphia, *circa* 1770, height 7¾in (19.6cm)
New York $5,500 (£2,683). 1.II.79

European Ceramics

An early Worcester coffee pot and cover, 1753–55, height $7\frac{1}{4}$in (18.4cm)
London £5,200 ($10,660). 24.X.78

A Worcester 'cabbage-leaf' jug, *circa* 1756, height 8in (20.3cm)
London £3,200 ($6,560). 24.X.78
From the collection of Mrs M. Joynson-Beaulieu

A pair of Bow monkey sweetmeat figures, *circa* 1755–60, height 5½in (14cm)
London £1,900 ($3,895). 3.VII.79

A pair of Chelsea partridge tureens and covers, 1752–56, width 5in (12.7cm)
London £2,800 ($5,740). 3.VII.79

A slipware charger by William Talor, late seventeenth century, diameter 17½in (44.5cm)
London £14,000($28,700). 24.X.78

Charles in the oak: a slipware dish by William Talor

Ronald Cooper

There exist, at present, one hundred and ten slip-decorated chargers of major importance made in Staffordshire during the second half of the seventeenth century. As less than ten remain in private collections, the sale last autumn of four dishes believed to have come originally from Bradgate House, home of Lady Jane Grey, was a notable event. One of these dishes, by William Talor, is discussed here (see opposite).

On 3 September 1651 Charles II was defeated by Cromwell's troops at Worcester. Long afterwards he related his escape to Samuel Pepys who recorded it in his diary:

> 'We carried up with us some victuals for the whole day, viz., bread, cheese, small beer and nothing else, and got up into a great oak . . . that could not be seen through and here we staid all day. While we were in this tree we see soldiers going up and down . . . searching for persons escaped, we seeing them, now and then . . . peeping out of the wood.'

After a series of extraordinary adventures, Charles succeeded in reaching France and remained in exile until 1660 when he returned triumphantly to England.

Domestic arts flourished during his reign and potters in Staffordshire (a Royalist area) responded to the current wave of patriotism by making a present total of thirty-nine dishes depicting royalty. These potters were William Talor, Ralph Simpson, Ralph Toft and Thomas Toft. The baptism of a William, son of William Talor, in August 1624 is recorded in the Burslem Parish Register, and the baptism of another William, son of Richard and Joan Talor in December 1632 is recorded in the Wolstanton Parish Register. Either of the above might be the potter who created this dish. There are thirteen signed by him and a further twelve, unsigned, identical in style. None of them is dated. Talor made more Royalist dishes than any of his contemporaries: four depict Charles in the oak, four show his coronation and the others illustrate crowned figures or courtiers.

As in the case of the other existing chargers this one is circular, wheel thrown and turned. It is made of coarse reddish-brown clay and decorated entirely with slip (clay diluted with water to the consistency of thin cream). White and brown clays occur naturally, black slip is obtained by adding manganese oxide to the brown. The upper surface of the dish is first coated with white slip. The decoration is then trailed on using brown and black, and the motifs are ornamented with multitudinous dots of

A slipware charger, probably by William Talor, late seventeenth century,
diameter 17in (43cm)
London £4,000($8,200). 24.X.78

white. After firing these earthy tones gleam under a honey-coloured lead glaze and
the rows of tiny white dots shine like stars.

Characteristic of William Talor's style is the very acute angle formed by the brown
and black strokes on the border and the amused tiny compact eyebrows on Charles's
face. His wig is ornamented with rosettes of minute dots – Talor was capable of the
most delicate slip trailing imaginable, especially when drawing hands. The lion's
cheeks are adorned with two amusing lollipop blobs of reddish-brown. A salient
feature of Talor's design is the 'Y' pattern formed by the two branches and the trunk,
which on other dishes he adapted to form a radial design (see above).

With reference to the story of Charles's elusion of enemy troops, his head is shown
in an oak tree flanked by the Royal Supporters, a lion and a unicorn. Like the cedar
and palm, the oak has been greatly venerated, a symbol of strength and longevity.
The isolated portrait head could be seen as a reminder of the martyrdom of Charles I as
much as of the resurrection of the monarchy under Charles II. Nevertheless it was
Charles II's escape and the subsequent cult of the Royal Oak which provided the
inspiration for this and other dishes within this group of slip-decorated Staffordshire
chargers which is unique in the history of ceramics.

A English delft polychrome posset pot and cover, inscribed *D.H.E.* and dated *1688/9*, height 15in (38cm)
London £4,200($8,610). 24.X.78

Two Nymphenburg figures, one of a Chinese lady with pineapples, and the other of a Chinaman with a teacup, modelled by Franz Anton Bustelli, marked with impressed shield, *circa* 1765, height of each 4¾in (12cm)
New York $7,000(£3,415); $11,500(£5,610). 8.III.79
From the collection of Fritz Katz

A Meissen group of *The Spanish lovers, Columbine and Beltrame*, modelled by J. J. Kaendler, *circa* 1741, height 7in (17.8cm)
London £8,000($16,400). 15.V.79
From the collection of Brigadier R. B. T. Daniell, DSO

A Meissen figure of Harlequin with a lorgnon, 1740–46, height $7\frac{1}{8}$ in (18cm)
New York $34,000 (£16,585). 8.III.79
From the collection of Fritz Katz

A Meissen Hausmaler armorial tankard with silver-gilt mounts, painted by Franz Ferdinand Mayer of Pressnitz, *circa* 1750, height 7⅛in (18cm)
New York $14,500(£7,073). 8.III.79

A Bayreuth Hausmaler beaker and saucer, possibly decorated by Johann Philipp Dannhöffer, *circa* 1737–43
London £5,000 ($10,250). 17.VII.79

A Meissen 'Watteau' tea and coffee service, marked with crossed swords in underglaze-blue, 1740–45, height of teapot $4\frac{1}{2}$in (11.5cm)
London £12,270 ($25,154). 15.V.79

A Hafner-ware tankard, late sixteenth century, height 13in (33cm)
London £9,400 ($19,270). 27.II.79
From the collection of the Vicomte de la Panouse

A Florentine albarello, inscribed *LUCRETIA*, late fifteenth century, height 11⅝in (29.5cm)
London £11,500 ($23,575). 15.V.79
Formerly in the Damiron Collection

An Urbino *istoriato* dish, dated *1546*, diameter 10½in (26.8cm)
New York $23,000 (£11,220). 6.VI.79
From the collection of the late Benjamin Sonnenberg

An Urbino *istoriato* dish, painted by Nicola Pellipario, *circa* 1530, diameter 12in (30.5cm)
London £25,000 ($51,250). 21.XI.78

An Eaas & Czjzcr 'Vienna' decorated plaque, painted by F. Wagner with a portrait of the Duchess of Devonshire after Gainsborough, late nineteenth century, diameter 19¾in (50.3cm)
Belgravia £3,000 ($6,150). 9.XI.78

A Berlin porcelain plaque, 1850–75,
height 12in (30.5cm)
PB Eighty-four $16,000 (£7,805). 25.X.78

A Meissen dinner and tea service, marked with crossed swords in underglaze-blue, early twentieth
century, diameter of dinner plate 9⅝in (25.4cm)
Belgravia £9,500 ($19,475). 9.XI.78

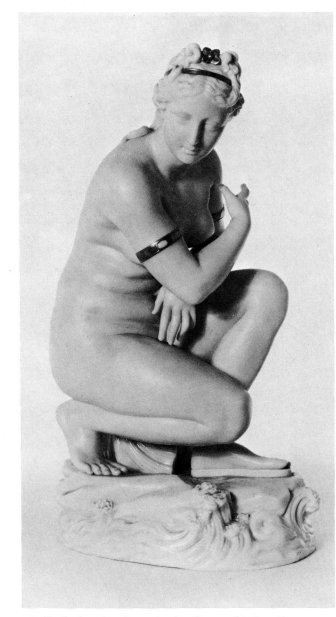

A Staffordshire commemorative mug made for the occasion of the proclamation of Queen Victoria, 1838, height 3½in (9cm)
Belgravia £520 ($1,066). 22.XI.78

A Belleek glazed and matt parian figure of Aphrodite, 1863–91, height 17in (43.2cm)
Belgravia £1,400 ($2,870). 14.VI.79

A Staffordshire bust of General Booth, *circa* 1900, height 14in (35.5cm)
Belgravia £480 ($984). 22.XI.78

A Royal Doulton 'Sung' vase by Charles Noke, *circa* 1925,
height 12½in (31.7cm)
Belgravia £900 ($1,845). 26. IV. 79

A Moorcroft 'Florian' vase, *circa*
1900, height 16½in (42cm)
Belgravia £550 ($1,128). 12.VII.79

A stoneware bottle vase by Bernard Leach,
impressed seal marks,
circa 1940, height $7\frac{3}{4}$in (19.6cm)
Belgravia £620($1,271). 12. VII.79

Left
A stoneware bottle vase by Shoji Hamada, *circa* 1960, height $9\frac{1}{8}$in (23.2cm)
Belgravia £1,800($3,690). 26.IV.79

Right
A stoneware vase by Bernard Leach, impressed *BL* and St Ives seals, *circa* 1930–35,
height 6in (15.2cm)
Belgravia £1,350($2,768). 26.IV.79

Art Nouveau and Art Deco

A writing cabinet by Charles Rennie Mackintosh, *circa* 1905, height 47⅝in (121cm)
Belgravia £80,000 ($164,000). 11.VII.79

This writing cabinet was originally conceived as part of the furnishings of Hill House, Helensburgh.
However, it was made for Mackintosh's own use and remained in his possession until his death

A gold, diamond, opal, enamel, hardstone and glass *parure de corsage* with a pendent pearl by
Georges Fouquet, Paris, *circa* 1900, with $7\frac{5}{8}$ in (19.5cm)
Monte Carlo FF200,000 (£21,978 : $45,055). 24.IX.78

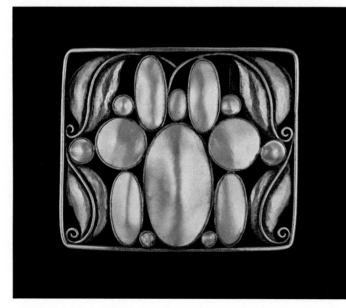

A Wiener Werkstatte silver-gilt and mother-of-
pearl buckle by Josef Hoffmann, *circa* 1910,
width $2\frac{1}{2}$ in (6.5cm)
Monte Carlo FF28,000 (£3,077:$6,308). 18.XI.78

A metal vase decorated with lacquer, part silvered and patinated by Jean Dunand,
Paris, *circa* 1925, height 24⅝in (62.5cm)
Monte Carlo FF165,000(£18,132:$37,170). 24.IX.78

A silver tea pot designed by Carlo Bugatti, maker's mark of A.A. Hébrard, Paris, *circa* 1910, height 9½in (24cm)
Belgravia £13,000 ($26,650). 8.XII.78

A Tiffany Favrile glass and bronze dragonfly lamp on a mosaic dragonfly base, maker's mark of Tiffany
Studios, New York, *circa* 1900, height 17½in (44.5cm)
New York $57,000 (£27,805). 31.III.79

An applied and internally-decorated glass marine vase by Emile Gallé, *circa* 1900, height 5in (12.7cm)
Monte Carlo FF140,000 (£15,385 : $31,538). 23.VI.79

Glass and Paperweights

A Venetian enamelled tazza, mid sixteenth century, diameter $10\frac{5}{8}$ in (27cm)
New York $8,000 (£3,902). 22.V.79

A pair of Baccarat close-millefiori tazze, signed, diameter of each 3¾in (9.5cm)
London £2,100($4,305). 2.VII.79

A Clichy flat-bouquet weight,
diameter 2$\frac{7}{8}$in (7.2cm)
London £2,900 ($5,945). 6.XI.78
From the collection of J. Warrell

A Clichy flower weight, diameter
2$\frac{3}{4}$in (7cm)
New York $3,600 (£1,756).
29.III.79

A Baccarat cruciform-bouquet weight,
diameter 3$\frac{5}{8}$in (9.2cm)
London £2,700 ($5,535). 6.XI.78
From the collection of J. Warrell

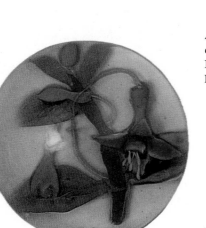

A fuchsia flower weight, diameter
3$\frac{1}{8}$in (8cm)
London £1,400 ($2,870). 6.XI.78

A St Louis dahlia flower weight,
diameter 3in (7.6cm)
New York $5,000 (£2,439). 29.III.79

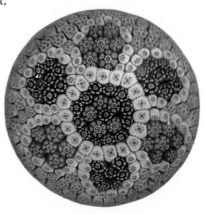

A Baccarat panelled carpet-ground
weight, diameter 2$\frac{7}{8}$in (7.2cm)
London £1,850 ($3,793). 6.XI.78
From the collection of J. Warrell

An engraved baluster goblet,
inscribed *Robert Buxton at the
Oxford Inn Exon, circa* 1720,
height 7⅛in (18.1cm)
London £500 ($1,025). 9.IV.79

In the Exeter archives Robert
Buxton is noted as being the
innkeeper of the Oxford Inn in a
case of arrest for unruly conduct
of a patron in 1726, and his death
is recorded in the parish records of
St David's, Exeter, in July 1750

The cross spider and *The great green grasshopper* from a set of six nineteenth-century goblets stipple-engraved and signed by Lawrence Whistler, *circa* 1950, height of each 5½ in (14cm)
Belgravia £900 ($1,845). 9.XI.78

A Venetian enamelled opalescent bowl from the Miotti Glasshouse, 1725–50, diameter $4\frac{7}{8}$in (12.5cm)
London £2,250 ($4,613). 21.V.79

Two gilt and enamelled wine glasses, *circa* 1745,
height of each $5\frac{1}{2}$in (14cm)
London £260 ($533); £340 ($697). 21.V.79

Clocks, Watches and Scientific Instruments

An ebony-veneered quarter-striking bracket clock by Joseph Knibb, London, *circa* 1675,
height 14in (35.5cm)
London £15,000 ($30,750). 15.XII.78
From the collection of Aileen Bridgewater

An ebony-veneered bracket clock by Tompion & Banger,
London, *circa* 1705, height 17in (43cm)
London £14,000 ($28,700). 15.XII.78

Above right
A George III rolling ball clock by William Congreve and
John Moxon, London, *circa* 1810, height 17in (43cm)
London £21,000 ($43,050). 30.III.79

A helical gearing month timepiece by Charles MacDowall,
Leeds, *circa* 1830, height 8¼in (21cm)
London £3,000 ($6,150). 15.XII.78

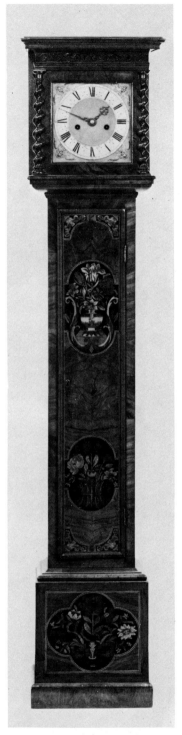

A walnut marquetry longcase
clock by John Wise, London,
circa 1680, height 6ft 8in (203cm)
London £5,000 ($10,250). 10.V.79
From the collection of the late
Frederick Poke

An inlaid mahogany longcase
clock by William Thompson,
Baltimore, 1799, height 8ft (244cm)
New York $7,000 (£3,415). 6.X.78
From the collection of the late
Nelson A. Rockefeller

A marquetry quarter-repeating
longcase clock by Joseph Antoni
Schoener, Augsburg, early
eighteenth century,
height 8ft 5in (258cm)
London £5,200 ($10,660). 6.X.78

A gilt-bronze band clock by Lenoir, inset with
porcelain plaques, Paris, *circa* 1860,
height 31in (79cm)
Belgravia £2,000 ($4,100). 20.VI.79

A Louis XV ormolu clock inset with gems and enamel plaques,
mid eighteenth century, height 16½in (42cm)
Geneva SFr 30,000 (£8,451:$17,324). 28.VI.79
From the Kanzler Collection

A German gilt-metal cased drum clock,
mid sixteenth century, diameter 1⅞in (4.8cm)
London £9,200 ($18,860). 1.XII.78
From the collection of Edward Hornby

A Japanese gilt-metal table clock,
nineteenth century, diameter 4½in (11.5cm)
London £20,000 ($41,000). 30.III.79
From the collection of the late P. L. Harrison

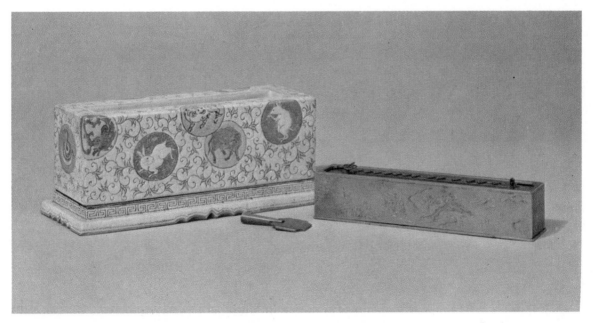

A Japanese paperweight clock by Fujiwara Tadanori, nineteenth century, length of case 5⅞in (15cm)
London £25,000 ($51,250). 30.III.79
From the collection of the late P. L. Harrison

Two views of a gilt-metal compendium for the English market by Christopher Schissler, Augsburg, dated *1556*, width 3in (7.6cm)
New York $34,000 (£16,585). 18.VI.79

A pocket globe by Johan Baptist Homann, Nuremberg, *circa* 1700, diameter 2¾in (7cm)
London £1,300 ($2,665). 30.III.79

A brass ring dial by George Adams, London, dated *1773*, diameter 11¾in (30cm)
London £3,300 ($6,765). 10.V.79

A universal achromatic telescope by Jesse Ramsden and
Peter Dolland, London, *circa* 1780, diameter of barrel
4in (10.2cm)
New York $15,000 (£7,317). 21.X.78

Above left
A parcel-gilt pedometer with perpetual calendar by
Hagar, Wolfenbuttel, 1696, width 2⅞in (7.4cm)
New York $9,000 (£4,390). 21.X.78
From the collection of Julius J. Bloch

A brass pocket microscope by John Clark, Edinburgh,
dated *1774*, width of box 4⅜in (11.2cm)
London £2,800 ($5,740). 14.VI.79

Fig 1
Two views of a silver-gilt watch in the form of a bird by C. Cameel, Strasbourg, *circa* 1630,
length $2\frac{7}{8}$in (7.3cm)
London £5,000 ($10,250). 1.XII.78

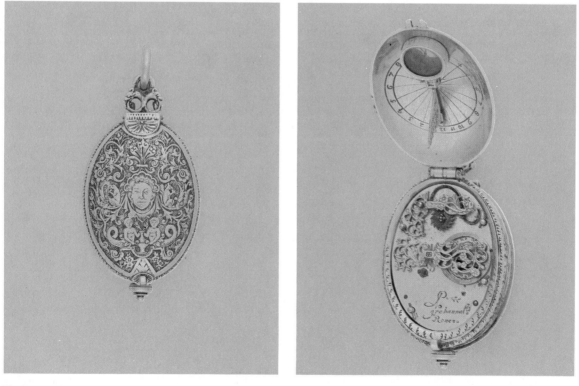

Fig 2
Two views of an oval gilt-metal verge watch by Pierre Grebauval, Rouen, *circa* 1615,
length $2\frac{1}{2}$in (6.5cm)
London £12,000 ($24,600). 1.XII.78

Watches from the Hornby Collection

George Daniels

Forty years ago very few people collected watches. Those who did, collected in a largely uncoordinated way and seem to have been motivated by curiosity and intuitive appreciation of fine quality work. Collectors with a profound knowledge of the history of watches were rare. As they had a virtually unlimited choice of every known maker, collections were large with examples of each stage of the development of the watch from 1500 to the late 1930s. The variety and range of the Edward Hornby Collection, begun in 1936, reflected this type of collection and would be hard to form again today.

Since the 1930s, and particularly during the last twenty years, the number of collectors has increased considerably. The inevitable reduction in watches available to each individual has resulted in a tendency to specialise in particular fields of horology. The vast amount of research undertaken and published during this period has assisted the process and watches which were once disregarded are now sought after and collected. This has meant the end of the large comprehensive collection and, in its place, the formation of many new smaller collections focusing on specific aspects of the development of the watch. The prices paid for watches at auction by today's collectors, who now recognise their value as historic and beautiful works of art, have brought just reward to the many who have instinctively preserved them from destruction, and especially from the gold vultures of the 1930s. Watches are never now bought for curiosity.

Essentially the purpose of a watch is to keep its owner informed of the time. One of the charms of the antique watch is that it can still be used for this purpose. Its accuracy will depend largely upon its period of manufacture and the philosophy of its maker.

The oldest watches that can be conveniently carried in the pocket are of early seventeenth-century manufacture. Their rate of going is somewhat capricious but they were used more as manifestations of personal wealth than as timekeepers. This aspect is reflected in their cases which are often curiously shaped and highly decorated. The silver-gilt case in the form of a bird by C. Cameel (Fig 1) is obviously intended to distract its owner's attention from its shortcomings as a timekeeper. In contrast Pierre Grebauval fitted a sun-dial into the back of the case of his oval watch so that, at least on fine days, the owner could be encouraged to set the watch to time and use it (Fig 2).

Fig 3
Two views of a gold and enamel cased verge watch by Francis Rainsford, London, *circa* 1700, diameter 1⅞in (4.8cm)
London £11,000 ($22,550). 1.XII.78

Fig 4
A gold and enamel verge watch by Nicolaus Rugendas, Augsburg, *circa* 1630, diameter 1⅜in (3.5cm)
London £7,800 ($15,990). 1.XII.78

Fig 5
A repoussé gold pair cased quarter-repeating verge watch, signed *Decharmes, London,* early eighteenth century, diameter 2⅛in (5.5cm)
London £3,500 ($7,175). 1.XII.78

Fig 6
A silver cased verge watch, signed with the monogram *IM* and inscribed *Richard Dashwood Esq. of Dearham Grange in Norfolk, circa 1690,* diameter 2in (5cm)
London £3,800 ($7,790). 1.XII.78

Fig 7
A silver cased verge watch with wandering hours by Anthoni Schmizt, Stuttgart, *circa* 1710, diameter 2in (5cm)
London £3,600 ($7,380). 1.XII.78

Left   Fig 8
JUSTIN VULLIAMY NO. ZON
A gold pair cased cylinder
watch, *circa* 1770, diameter
2⅛in (5.5cm)
London £2,100 ($4,305).
1.XII.78

Right   Fig 9
THOMAS MUDGE & WILLIAM
DUTTON NO. 832
A gold pair cased cylinder
watch, 1759, diameter 2⅛in
(5.5cm)
London £1,500 ($3,075).
1.XII.78

Such watches may vary their timekeeping by half an hour in twelve. This might seem to be a preposterous rate of error but only the obsessive could fail to enjoy the sound of their frantic determination to succeed. Charles I drove himself to distraction trying to make all his timekeepers agree on the hour of the day, but he was a notably obsessive man. Alexander Pope understood the whimsicalities of watches and the difficulties of their makers. In sensing their determination to be helpful he offered encouragement with the view, 'Tis with our judgments as our watches, none go just alike, yet each believes his own'. This sentiment is not inappropriate to the philosophy of the modern collector.

Because the watchmaker was unable to improve the performance of his watches, case decoration was his principal occupation almost until the end of the seventeenth century. As a consequence the period is rich in variety of type and style of ornament. Enamel cases are much in demand today and the polychrome allegorical scenes and landscapes of Francis Rainsford (Fig 3) and the stylised floral decoration of the watch by Nicolaus Rugendas (Fig 4) represent extremes of this type.

With the introduction of the balance spring to control the vibrations of the balance, timekeeping of the watch improved. Anxious to demonstrate his new capabilities the watchmaker turned his attention to methods of indicating the new rates of time-keeping. The maker of the silver watch signed *IM* (Fig 6) was one of the first to use two hands to indicate hours and minutes separately as was later universally adopted. The use of a seconds hand also was an extremely bold step which the watch was not sufficiently accurate to justify. One of the most popular methods of indicating hours and minutes was used by Anthoni Schmizt (Fig 7). This was the wandering hour dial copied from English makers. The hour appears in a window which travels within the half-circle aperture to indicate the minutes at the edge. When the sixty-minute mark is reached the next following hour appears and the action is repeated.

The appearance of enamel dials in the early eighteenth century heralded a simpler style of watch as exemplified by the work of Thomas Mudge & William Dutton (Fig 9) and Justin Vulliamy (Fig 8). Cases were often in gold or silver repoussé and classical scenes, such as that on the verge watch by Decharmes (Fig 5), were popular.

Fig 10
L. GOLAY NO. 18642
A gold cased *grande et petite sonnerie* clock-watch with repetition at will, mid nineteenth century, diameter 2⅜in (6.1cm)
London £6,200 ($12,710).
1.XII.78

Fig 11
RECORDON NO. 180
A silver cased self-winding watch, 1794, diameter 2⅛in (5.5cm)
London £6,200 ($12,710).
1.XII.78

Fig 12
JOHN ARNOLD NO. 39/88
A gold cased half quarter dumb repeating chronometer, 1782, diameter 3in (7.5cm)
London £12,000 ($24,600).
1.XII.78

It is usual to associate watches with Switzerland but in fact the Swiss made little contribution to the watch until the late nineteenth century when they began to mass-produce watches by machine methods. The best Swiss makers found it necessary to bring their watches to London for sale or have them made in London. The extremely rare self-winding watch by Recordon (Fig 11) is an example of a watch made partly in Switzerland and partly in London by a Swiss resident in London. The fine, large gold clock-watch by Golay (Fig 10) illustrates the quality of work done by the best Swiss makers in the mid nineteenth century. It strikes the hours and quarters in passing, and by pressing a button in the pendant will repeat the last hour and quarter.

The second half of the eighteenth century saw a remarkable improvement in the performance of English watches. Some, especially developed for precise timekeeping, can maintain a rate within a few seconds per day and are wholly suitable for modern use. This takes no account of the value of the watch which may range from a few hundred to many thousands of pounds. But a watch is a living thing and a collector who is a student of his subject will choose from his collection a watch to carry and enjoy each day, irrespective of its value. Not many fields of art can offer such consolation to the collector as he contemplates the curious beauty of his watch while seeking escape from the more pressing parts of the twentieth-century day.

The development of the high precision timekeeper was by no means accidental. It was the direct outcome of an Act of Parliament offering a reward of £20,000 for the discovery of a means of determining longitude at sea. This was a huge sum of money and was no doubt offered on the principle that the way to distract a professional from earning his living and persuade him to exploit his talents is to offer him the chance of becoming rich.

In the end the prize was won by the Yorkshire-born carpenter, John Harrison, who, by original thinking supported by the dour tenacity of his breed, succeeded in producing a timekeeper that fulfilled the requirements of the Act. These were so loosely drawn up that the Lords of the Admiralty, who were the judges of the entries, were little better off because Harrison's machine was so complicated as to be unsuitable for general manufacture. But an important aspect of the work was his demonstration of the capabilities of the timekeeper in determining the longitude. With this in mind the profession, led by John Arnold, set to work, along different lines, to produce a form of timekeeper that assisted the navigator to expand British trade abroad and help found the wealth and influence of the nation. For quite different reasons the watches by John Arnold (Fig 12) are equally prized by their present owners.

Although the Englishman was willing to pace his life by the demands of the precision watch the Frenchman disdained such shackles. He preferred to believe that he himself dictated the pace of his affairs. His more fanciful horological requirements were satisfied by the Swiss-born A. L. Breguet who knew exactly how to exploit the French preference for novelty. He made watches of every kind but is perhaps best known for his *montres perpetuelles* (Fig 14) which wind themselves automatically while carried in the pocket. He first made examples for Marie Antoinette and the Duc d'Orléans, and this encouraged their purchase by anyone who could afford the luxury of an expensive status symbol. They are still regarded by some, including the writer, as the utmost perfection in watches. In addition to their convenience in daily wear they are repeaters and so are equally useful at night.

Breguet's ability to invent a watch to cater for every market made him the richest and most celebrated maker of his day. An interesting innovation is seen in his *montres souscription* (Fig 13), so called because the purchaser assisted their construction with a down payment to finance the cost of tools and materials needed after the devastation of his workshop during the French Revolution. Although the *souscriptions* have only one hand, there is no difficulty in telling the time to within two minutes. Their mixed silver and gold cases and simple white enamel dials typify Breguet's elegant style.

With his *montres à tact* (Fig 15), the time can be found by feeling the position of the hand relative to touch pieces at the edge of the chapter ring. These are sometimes called blind man's watches, but a repeating watch would be easier to use and much cheaper, for the prices of *montres à tact* bear no relationship to the simplicity of their

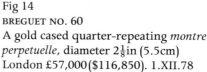

Fig 14
BREGUET NO. 60
A gold cased quarter-repeating *montre
perpetuelle*, diameter 2⅛in (5.5cm)
London £57,000 ($116,850). 1.XII.78

Fig 13
BREGUET NO. 3808
A gold cased *montre souscription*,
diameter 2⅜in (6.2cm)
London £8,000 ($16,400). 1.XII.78

Fig 15
BREGUET NO. 3561
A gold cased *montre à tact*,
diameter 2in (5cm)
London £8,000 ($16,400). 1.XII.78

construction. It was the opinion of the 7th Duke of Wellington that such watches were worn principally by dandies who wished surreptitiously to discover if they could decently quit their host and seek fresh amusement in other places. Breguet would undoubtedly know what price to put on such a treasure. His work still commands the highest prices and it is a sobering thought that the Breguet *perpetuelle* sold for exactly twice the original cost of the whole collection.

It is interesting, since no great value was attached to watches, that they should have survived in such large numbers. This could be because a watch is a very personal thing and plays a continuous part in its owner's affairs. It is therefore easily accepted as an heirloom with direct personal connections and will be treasured and preserved. Today, however, another factor helps its survival – the near impossibility of having a modern equivalent made. The watch collector now realises that he is preserving the beauty of an art that may disappear for ever, an art that combined aesthetic, intellectual, scientific and practical qualities in a unique way.

A Swiss gold and enamel open-faced quarter-repeating erotic automaton watch, *circa* 1820, diameter 2¼in (5.6cm)
New York $29,000 (£14,146). 21.X.78

A gold and enamel self-winding centre seconds clock-watch by Jaquet Droz, London, *circa* 1790, diameter 2⅛in (5.5cm)
London £26,500 ($54,325). 1.XII.78
From the collection of Edward Hornby

A gold and enamel open-faced minute-repeating split-seconds chronograph by Patek, Philippe & Co, Geneva, 1913, diameter 2⅛in (5.5cm)
New York $35,000 (£17,073). 13.XII.78

A gold hunting cased keyless chronometer tourbillon by Paul Ditisheim, dated *1903–13*, diameter 2¼in (5.6cm)
London £25,000 ($51,250). 15.XII.78

A Swiss gold and enamel open-faced rose-form musical automaton watch, *circa* 1820, diameter 2in (5cm)
New York $59,000 (£28,780). 21.X.78

Above left
A Swiss gold and enamel quarter-repeating open-faced watch set with jewels, *circa* 1820, diameter $2\frac{1}{8}$in (5.5cm)
$21,000(£10,244)

Above right
A gold and enamel open-faced watch by William Ilbery, London, *circa* 1800, diameter $2\frac{3}{8}$in (6cm)
$26,000(£12,683)

Centre
A Swiss gold and enamel quarter-repeating musical watch, *circa* 1810, length 4in (10.2cm)
$50,000(£24,390)

Below
A pair of Swiss silver-gilt and enamel open-faced watches, *circa* 1820, diameter $2\frac{1}{2}$in (6.4cm)
$20,000(£9,756)

The watches on this page were sold in New York on 18 June 1979

Jewellery

A pearl and diamond stomacher designed as a fountain of honeysuckle scrolls,
circa 1910
London £160,000 ($328,000). 26.X.78

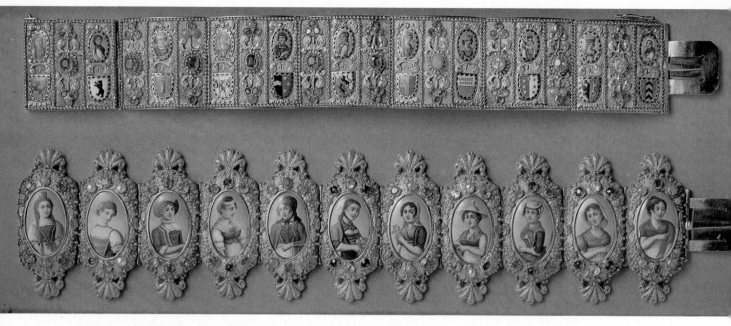

Above A gold bracelet set with Geneva enamel miniatures and gems, *circa* 1830
London £3,100 ($6,355). 28.IX.78
Below A gold bracelet set with Geneva enamel miniatures and gems, *circa* 1820
London £3,200 ($6,560). 28.IX.78

Opposite
An emerald and diamond pendant in the form of a Latin cross, *circa* 1840
London £38,000 ($77,900). 12.IV.79

A gold, black opal and jewelled necklace by Tiffany & Co, *circa* 1890
PB Eighty-four $20,000 (£9,756). 10.IV.79
From the collection of the late Margaret Kurtz

Above A gold, enamel, lapis lazuli and jade vanity case by La Cloche Frères,
SFr13,000(£3,662:$7,507)
Left An emerald (8.18 carats) and diamond ring, SFr240,000(£67,606:$138,592)
Centre A black onyx, coral and diamond jabot pin by Boucheron, SFr11,000(£3,099:$6,352)
Right An ivory, sapphire and diamond clip, SFr5,000(£1,408:$2,886)
Below The clasp and hoop of an evening bag by Gerard Sandos, SFr10,000(£2,817:$5,775)

The jewellery on this page was sold in St Moritz on 16 February 1979

Above An enamel, pearl and diamond plaque brooch, *circa* 1925, £1,900 ($3,895)
Centre A Russian ruby and diamond brooch, *circa* 1900, £1,300 ($2,665)
Below A diamond brooch pendant, £8,200 ($16,810)
Left and right A pair of turquoise and diamond pendent earrings, *circa* 1910, £850 ($1,743)

The jewellery on this page was sold in London on 24 May 1979

A ruby and diamond necklace by Cartier, *circa* 1920
New York $660,000 (£321,951). 5.IV.79

Above left An emerald-cut diamond ring by Van Cleef & Arpels, the diamond weighing 5.8 carats
SFr240,000 (£67,606:$138,592)
Above right A rectangular step-cut diamond ring, the diamond weighing 15.82 carats
SFr690,000 (£194,366:$398,451)
Centre An emerald and diamond bracelet, SFr52,000 (£14,648:$30,028)
Below A diamond, coloured stone and enamel pendant by La Cloche Frères
SFr62,000 (£17,465:$35,803)

The jewellery on this page was sold in Zurich on 21 November 1978

Above left A pair of diamond earclips by Cartier, the pear-shaped diamonds weighing approximately 32.5 carats, $580,000 (£282,927)
From the collection of the late Joan Whitney Payson
Above right A platinum and diamond necklace, the pear-shaped diamond weighing approximately 2 carats, $45,000 (£21,951)
Centre A marquise-shaped diamond ring, the diamond weighing 12.06 carats, $425,000 (£207,317)
Below A platinum and diamond bracelet, the marquise-shaped diamonds weighing a total of 21 carats, $72,500 (£35,366)

The jewellery on this page was sold in New York on 4 April 1979

Above A diamond pendent necklace, the two yellow old-mine diamonds weighing approximately 21.25 carats and 4.15 carats
$70,000 (£34,146)
Below A gold, platinum and diamond necklace by Black, Starr & Frost, the central old-mine diamond weighing approximately 5.85 carats, *circa* 1900
$210,000 (£102,439)

The jewellery on this page is from the collection of the late Olyve Graef Moore and was sold in New York on 19 October 1978

1. An alexandrite (4.98 carats) and diamond ring, Hong Kong HK$58,000(£5,524:$11,324). 28.V.79
2. A black opal (13.02 carats), Hong Kong HK$130,000(£12,381:$25,381). 28.V.79
3. A ruby (5.68 carats) and diamond ring, Hong Kong HK$280,000(£26,667:$54,667). 1.XII.78
4. A diamond (11.59 carats) and sapphire ring, New York $310,000(£151,220). 4.IV.79
5. An alexandrite (approx 20.5 carats) and diamond ring, Zurich SFr125,000(£35,211:$72,183). 22.XI.78
6. A ruby (approx 3.75 carats) and diamond ring by C.D. Peacock, New York $90,000(£43,902). 6.XII.78
7. An emerald (1 carat) and diamond ring, Hong Kong HK$65,000(£6,190:$12,690). 1.XII.78
8. A sapphire (approx 8 carats) and diamond ring, New York $130,000(£63,415). 5.IV.79
9. A sapphire (approx 8.5 carats) and diamond ring, Hong Kong HK$125,000(£11,905:$24,405). 28.V.79
10. A sapphire (approx 11.85 carats) and diamond ring by Charlton, *circa* 1920, New York $140,000(£68,293). 18.X.78
11. A sapphire (approx 12 carats) and diamond ring, New York $150,000(£73,171). 6.XII.78
12. A step-cut emerald (7.65 carats), London £60,000($123,000). 26.X.78
13. A jade and diamond ring, Hong Kong HK$210,000(£20,000:$41,000). 1.XII.78
14. An emerald (approx 2.15 carats) and diamond ring, New York $56,000(£27,317). 7.XII.78
15. An emerald (approx 6.35 carats) and diamond ring by Tiffany & Co, New York $110,000(£53,659). 6.XII.78
16. A star ruby (23.98 carats) and diamond ring, Hong Kong HK$38,000(£3,619:$7,419). 1.XII.78

A star ruby and diamond ring, the ruby weighing 42.97 carats
Hong Kong HK$170,000 (£16,190:$33,190).
1.XII.78

An alexandrite and diamond lavaliere by Beatties & Sons, the alexandrite weighing approximately 22.3 carats
New York $145,000 (£70,732). 19.X.78

An emerald and diamond brooch by J.E. Caldwell & Co, the emerald weighing approximately 2.25 carats, *circa* 1930
New York $41,000 (£20,000). 18.X.78
From the collection of Ann K. Johnson

A star sapphire and diamond ring, the sapphire weighing 75.7 carats
Hong Kong HK$310,000 (£29,524:$60,524).
28.V.79

A diamond necklace by Chaumet, SFr650,000 (£183,099:$375,352)
A diamond brooch, SFr285,000 (£80,282:$164,578)

The jewellery on this page was sold in Zurich on 16 May 1979

Above and below A diamond brooch with matching earclips, SFr320,000 (£90,141:$184,789)
Centre A ruby and diamond bracelet by Van Cleef & Arpels, SFr320,000 (£90,141:$184,789)

The jewellery on this page was sold in St Moritz on 16 February 1979

A diamond and sapphire necklace in the shape of morning glories by Tiffany & Co
New York $24,000 (£11,707). 24.V.79

Coins and Medals

ROMAN, aureus of Diadumenian (217–218 AD)
London £26,000 ($53,300). 20.VI.79
From the collection of Patrick A. Doheny

Marcus Opelius Diadumenianus, son of the Emperor Macrinus, was raised to the rank of
Caesar at the age of nine; the following year, however, saw the defeat of his father by
Elagabalus and he himself was executed whilst fleeing to Parthia

Fig 1
ROMAN, aureus of Pertinax
(January – March 193 AD)
London £6,400 ($13,120). 20.VI.79

Fig 2
ROMAN, aureus of Didius Julianus
(March – June 193 AD)
London £10,000 ($20,500).
20.VI.79

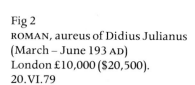

Fig 3
ROMAN, aureus of Manlia
Scantilla, wife of Didius Julianus,
193 AD
London £9,000 ($18,450). 20.VI.79

Fig 4
ROMAN, aureus of Septimius
Severus (193 – 211 AD) with a bust
of his wife, Julia Domna, on the
reverse
London £7,200 ($14,760). 20.VI.79

The Doheny Collection of ancient coins

Thomas Eden

Patrick A. Doheny formed his collection in the 1950s and early '60s, largely from the major sales of that period. Whilst it included a splendid series of Greek coins it will undoubtedly be best remembered for its Roman section, and in particular for the group of seventy aurei which contained many rare examples of the lesser-known emperors and empresses. Collectors are always interested in the historical back-ground to coins and the circumstances surrounding one such emperor, Didius Julianus, were particularly unusual.

Following the death of Commodus in 192 AD, the Praetorian guard chose Pertinax, the prefect of the city, as emperor. The collection included a fine example of his gold coinage with the reverse legend reading *PROVID DEOR*, an allusion to his godlike qualities (Fig 1). Ironically, however, it was these qualities which led to reforms and economies that were his eventual downfall and the Praetorians themselves were responsible for his murder after a reign of only eighty-six days.

Next took place one of the most extraordinary events in Roman history, the Praetorians offered the empire to the highest bidder in what must surely have been the most bizarre auction ever held. As history relates, two men took up the bidding, Sulpicianus, the governor of the City of Rome and Didius Julianus, a wealthy senator. Gibbon in *The Decline and Fall of the Roman Empire* states:

> 'The vain old man [Julianus] hastened to the Praetorian camp where Sulpicianus was still in treaty with the guards; and began to bid against him from the foot of the rampart. The unworthy negotiation was transacted by faithful emissaries who passed alternately from one candidate to the other.'

Finally Julianus outbid his opponent, offering 25,000 sestertii for each soldier of the guard, and was duly elected emperor. However, the circumstances of his election infuriated the people of Rome and appeals were sent to the rulers of the provinces not only to avenge Pertinax's murder but also to depose the present emperor. Julianus attempted negotiations but after a reign of only sixty-six days, was finally beheaded by Septimius Severus, the governor of Pannonia.

As might be expected of so short-lived an emperor, his coins, particularly in gold, are very rare and the aureus in the Doheny Collection (which depicted the goddess Fortuna on the reverse!) aroused great interest (Fig 2). Furthermore the collection included even rarer gold coins of his wife, Manlia Scantilla (Fig 3), and his daughter, Didia Clara, together with several examples of his successor, Septimius Severus (Fig 4).

SWEDEN, Stockholm mint, 2 riksdalers of Johann III (1568–92)
London £950 ($1,948). 24.I.79

EGYPT, 500 guerche of 'Abd al Aziz, regnal year 11 (1871)
London £10,000 ($20,500). 12.X.78

TURKEY, 500 piastres of Mohammed V, regnal year 2
(1911), for the royal visit to Edirne
London £2,300 ($4,715). 25.IV.79

ANCIENT GREEK, Syracuse dekadrachm by Kimon,
circa 400 BC
London £6,400 ($13,120). 18.VII.79
From the collection of the late Norman Colville

ROMAN, aureus of Julia Domna
(died 217 AD)
London £5,200 ($10,660). 28.III.79
From the collection of His Highness
Prince Sadruddin Aga Khan

ROMAN, solidus of Constantine
II Caesar (317–337 AD)
London £1,800 ($3,690). 28.III.79
From the collection of His Highness
Prince Sadruddin Aga Khan

ENGLAND, London mint, noble of Henry IV
(1399–1413), second light issue
London £2,200 ($4,510). 13.XII.78

FLANDERS, lion d'or of Louis de Male (1346–84)
London £2,200 ($4,510). 19.X.78

SARDINIA, 5 doppia of Charles Emanuel III, 1755
London £5,200 ($10,660). 13.XII.78

ENGLAND, shilling of Charles II, 1666,
elephant below bust
London £2,000 ($4,100). 19.X.78

ENGLAND, pattern broad of Oliver
Cromwell, 1656
London £4,500 ($9,225). 23.V.79

IRELAND, copper farthing issued during
the Seige of Cork (1645–47)
London £1,100 ($2,255). 19.X.78

NETHERLANDS, paper quarter-gulden issued
during the Seige of Leyden (1573–74)
London £200 ($410). 23.V.79

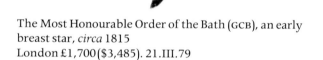

Queen's Messenger's badge
(Victoria), awarded to John Cooper,
War Department, 1854
London £580 ($1,189). 27.IX.78

The Most Honourable Order of the Bath (GCB), an early
breast star, *circa* 1815
London £1,700 ($3,485). 21.III.79

Prince of Wales' visit to India
(1875–76), presentation gold medal
awarded to His Highness The
Maharana of Dholepore
London £2,500 ($5,125). 21.III.79

Collectors' Sales

An 'Alsatian' coal and smokeless fuel closed stove by F. Küppersbusch, German, *circa* 1910, height 43½in (110.5cm)
Belgravia £3,800 ($7,790). 7.III.79

A 'Spider' stream-driven
carriage by Bing, German,
circa 1899, length 9in (23cm)
Belgravia £3,100 ($6,355).
6.X.78

A New York Central system 408E 0-4-4-0 engine and a Minneapolis St Paul
class electric 381-E 4-4-4 engine from a six-piece Lionel standard gauge
'State' set, *circa* 1930, approximate length of each 17in (43.2cm)
PB Eighty-four $8,500 (£4,146). 6.XII.78

An AMI model 'A' 'mother of plastic' 78 rpm juke box, American, *circa* 1946, height 70in (178cm)
Belgravia £1,500 ($3,075). 23.III.79

A folding stereo camera by Horne & Thornthwaite, English, *circa* 1880
Belgravia £3,800 ($7,790). 2.III.79

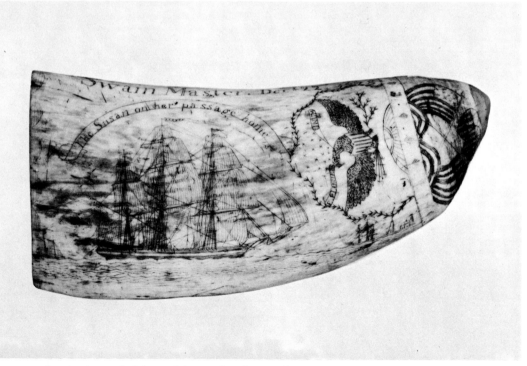

An engraved scrimshaw whale's tooth by Frederick Myrick, inscribed *The Ship Susan, Frederick Swain Master, Dec. 22nd 1828* and *The Maria Islands*, American, length 6½in (16.5cm)
New York $29,000 (£14,146). 23.VI.79

A 'screaming' Jumeau musical
automaton of a young girl
holding a broken puppet,
probably by Lambert, height
of figure 15½in (39.4cm)
PB Eighty-four $8,500 (£4,146).
6.XII.78

A George III carved and painted
wooden doll, *circa* 1770, height
23in (58.4cm)
Belgravia £1,750 ($3,588). 11.V.79

A French socketed bisque fashion doll,
circa 1860, height 18in (45.8cm)
Belgravia £1,800 ($3,690). 20.XII.79

Fig 1
A view of Stewart Gregory's home in Connecticut, showing some of the major pieces in his collection

The Gregory Collection of American folk art

Robert Bishop

Folk art is the art of the common man, and was fashioned by untutored artisans without the benefit of formal training. Many of these craftsmen were inspired by the desire to transform what was purely utilitarian into something more beautiful or decorative. They used their talent, sense of humour, and, more essentially, their hearts in their creative efforts. Most folk art pieces were made by hand and grew out of surviving European craft traditions transplanted to the American colonies by settlers. Paintings, textiles, weathervanes and small decorative carvings are typical of this work.

All of these categories, with the exception of textiles, were represented in the American folk art collection of the late Stewart E. Gregory (1913–76). A man of refined tastes, Gregory was a graduate of Princeton and Harvard, and also studied at Cambridge University. In 1945 he moved from New York to Wilton, Connecticut, where he acquired a large barn which had been in his family for many years. It was this building that inspired his interest in American folk art and once remodelled it served both as his home and the setting for his dazzling collection (Fig 1). Although Gregory was an ambitious and knowledgeable collector, he frequently relied upon the assistance of recognised experts in the field. Mary Allis, a distinguished dealer from Southport, Connecticut, often advised him on the acquisition of paintings and weathervanes. Adele Earnest of Stony Point, New York, helped him select American waterfowl decoys of great sculptural beauty and distinction.

While some viewed the interest in the sale of the Gregory Collection as the beginning of a broad appreciation of the arts created by the common man, many saw it as the summit of the gradually rising acceptance of American folk art as a legitimate art form. They look to the past and point out convincingly that interest in material of this type really began in 1924 with a small exhibition titled 'Early American art' at the Whitney Studio Club in New York. This was followed by three more important exhibitions in the '30s, all of them consisting largely of loans from the private collection of Abby Aldrich Rockefeller. As interest in folk art continued to grow after the war, museum exhibitions, culminating in 'The flowering of American folk art' at the Whitney Museum in 1976, directed national attention towards the contributions of America's naive artists.

Fig 2
A moulded copper weathervane of the Indian Mashamoquet, nineteenth century,
height 45in (114.4cm)
New York $25,000 (£12,195). 27.I.79

Stewart Gregory had been particularly demanding about the pieces he added to his collection and had always sought the best possible examples both in terms of condition and from an aesthetic point of view. It is not surprising, therefore, that at the sale there were more than eighteen individual record prices and that top sums were paid for naive paintings, weathervanes and carved figures, which were the main focus of the collection.

Weathervanes have been part of the American landscape since the early seventeenth century and often appear on maps of that period. Although they were first based on European models, American craftsmen soon created their own designs inspired by indigenous motifs. The vigour, imagination and inventiveness displayed in these works have led many people to consider them to be the first form of native American sculpture. The most outstanding among many fine examples in the Gregory Collection, was a nineteenth-century moulded copper representation of the Indian Mashamoquet (Fig 2) who was chief of the Nitmuck tribe. The vane originally adorned a building in Pomfret, Connecticut, which is adjacent to the Mashamoquet State Park. Collectors prefer copper vanes to be unrestored, retaining the patina acquired over the years, and this one was distinctive in this respect.

Fig 3
DEBORAH GOLDSMITH
Mr and Mrs Lyman Day
Watercolour, New York, *circa* 1823, 9in by 8¾in (22.8cm by 22cm)
New York $29,000 (£14,146). 27.I.79

Fig 4
A carved and painted wood bust of Captain
M. Starbuck, dated on the scrimshaw plaque
Nantucket 1838, height 13¾in (35cm)
New York $30,000 (£14,634). 27.I.79

Fig 5
A carved and painted
wood lectern box,
inscribed *P.F. Coist*,
New England, 1860–75,
width 13½in (34.2cm)
New York $17,000
(£8,293). 27.I.79

Fig 6
JOHN BREWSTER JR
Portrait of a child
Mounted on aluminium, 38in by 25⅛in (96.5cm by 64cm)
New York $67,500 (£32,927). 27.I.79

Fig 7
AMMI PHILLIPS
Portrait of a lady
One of a pair, *circa* 1836,
31¼in by 26¼in (79.5cm by 66.7cm)
New York $62,500 (£30,488). 27.I.79

The wood-carving section included a lectern box used for holding a bible (Fig 5) and an imposing bust of Captain M. Starbuck (Fig 4). The bust was typical, on a small scale, of a certain type of marine carving of which figureheads are the best-known examples. Throughout the seventeenth and early eighteenth centuries figureheads on American ships generally followed English prototypes and were in the form of 'lyons' and other beasts, but by the 1760s human figures, often symbolising the vessel's name, had become popular. This bust was doubtless a portrait of the ship's captain and would probably have stood in one of the cabins.

Folk painting depends on broad, flat areas of colour and a strong sense of design instead of the technical perfection of its academic counterpart, but, as Maxim Karolik has noted, 'Its lack of ability to describe does not hamper its ability to express'. It also frequently provides documentary evidence for the furnishings of early American homes and the watercolour, *Mr and Mrs Lyman Day* (Fig 3), showed the bright, patterned wall and floor coverings popular in the 1820s. There was also a flowered rug in the *Child in a green dress* (Fig 8) by J. Bradley, who was working some twenty years later. Ammi Phillips, the most renowned of American folk artists, worked for an extraordinarily long period of time and like many other New England limners used several styles during his career. His early work was neo-classical in appearance. He

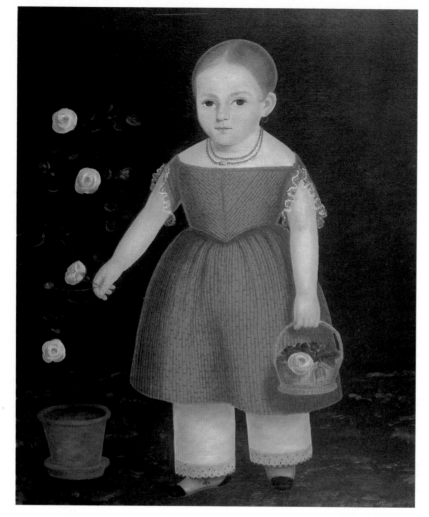

Fig 8
J. BRADLEY
Child in a green dress
Signed and inscribed *128 Spring Street,
New York, circa* 1840, 33in by 26in
(83.8cm by 66cm)
New York $43,000(£20,976). 27.I.79

depicted his sitters in Empire-style dress and used mainly light, pastel shades. At the
end of his life his portraits became highly individualised showing the character of the
sitter, but were rather sombre. The work of the middle period, therefore, struck a
balance between the idealisation of the early neo-classical style and the more subdued
palette of his late years. The pair of portraits owned by Gregory (Fig 7) demonstrated
this perfectly and these two paintings are widely considered to be the best examples
of Phillips's middle period work. John Brewster Jr, a near contemporary of Phillips's,
is especially noted for his portraits of children. Typical of his work was the example
in the Gregory Collection with its striking pose and geometric floor pattern (Fig 6).

   During his lifetime Stewart Gregory established a reputation as a discerning
collector, strict about the quality of his acquisitions. At the same time his charm and
humour were reflected in his choice of objects. It was these two factors that made this
an exceptional collection, and the interest generated by its dispersal confirmed that
the value and importance of American folk art has finally been recognised.

Postage Stamps

UNITED STATES OF AMERICA, 1898 Trans-Mississippi $2 plate block with imprint
New York $85,000(£41,463). 9.V.79

UNITED STATES OF AMERICA, 1847 5c pair on hand-coloured fancy envelope,
probably a Valentine
London £9,000($18,450). 30.III.79

UNITED STATES OF AMERICA, 1894 50c orange block of sixteen
Los Angeles $12,000(£5,854). 9.IV.79

GREAT BRITAIN, 1883–84 5s crimson corner
block of four
London £3,000($6,150). 26.X.78

RHODESIA, 1910–13
£1 perforated 15
London £3,400 ($6,970).
24.XI.78
From the collection of the
late S.D. Cramer

CEYLON, 1912–25 500 rupees
London £2,600 ($5,330).
23.XI.78
From the collection of the late
S.D. Cramer

RHODESIA, 1910–13
£1 error of colour
London £3,200 ($6,560).
24.XI.78
From the collection of the
late S.D. Cramer

SOUTH AFRICA,
1913–24 £1 with plate
number
Johannesburg R 1,500
(£857:$1,757). 2.IV.79

SOUTH WEST AFRICA, 1923 £1 block of
four, the upper left stamp without
full stop after 'Afrika'
London £3,600 ($7,380). 24.XI.78
From the collection of the late
S.D. Cramer

NYASALAND, 1913–18 £10
London £1,100 ($2,255).
24.XI.78
From the collection of
the late S.D. Cramer

NEW GUINEA, 1914 GRI
5s on 5 mark
London £2,000 ($4,100).
24.XI.78
From the collection of the
late S.D. Cramer

RHODESIA, 1917 Livingstone provisional
horizontal pair with inverted surcharge, the
right stamp with the spaced 'nn' variety
Johannesburg R 11,000 (£6,286:$12,886).
29.VI.79

CAMEROONS (British
Occupation), 1915 3s on 3
mark, variety double
surcharge
London £750 ($1,538).
23.XI.78
From the collection of the
late S.D. Cramer

Photographs

EDWARD STEICHEN
Lotus, Mount Kisco, New York
Silver print mounted on card, signed, 1915, $9\frac{5}{8}$in by $7\frac{5}{8}$in (24.5cm by 19.4cm)
New York $4,500 (£2,195). 8.V.79

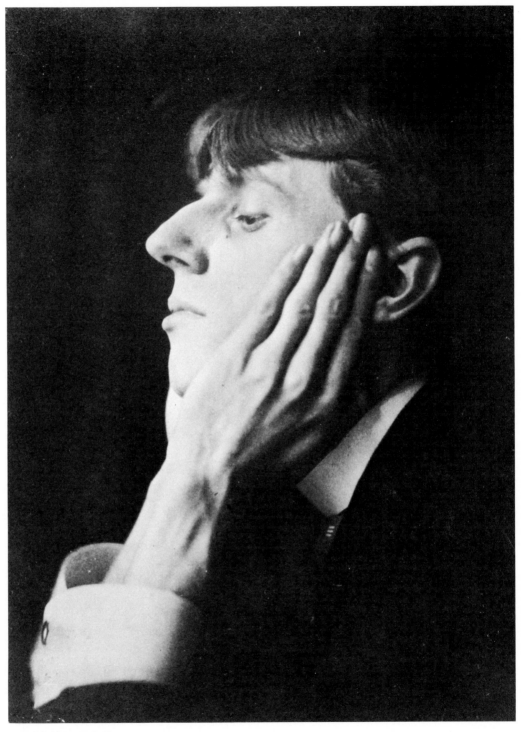

FREDERICK H. EVANS
One of two portraits of Aubrey Beardsley
Platinum print in presentation folder, 1895, 5$\frac{3}{8}$in by 3$\frac{7}{8}$in (13.6cm by 9.8cm)
Belgravia £1,800($3,690). 29.VI.79

A Dutch silver-mounted
corkscrew, *circa* 1850
London £350 ($718). 22.V.79

An F. A. Whelan's 1881 patent
corkscrew
London £255 ($523). 29.IX.78

From left to right
Château Lafite 1848 (one bottle), bottled by the Café Voisin, Paris; London £320 ($656). 29.IX.78
Tokay *circa* 1680–1700 with the arms of the Electors of Saxony seal (one small bottle); London
£1,300 ($2,665). 13.XII.78
Elixir Végétal de la Grande Chartreuse Grandeur no 2 (one small bottle); London £130 ($267). 22.V.79
Château d'Yquem 1858 (one bottle); London £665 ($1,363). 22.V.79
Vieux Cognac 1811 with 'Comet' seal (one magnum); London £520 ($1,066). 29.IX.78

Wine Sales

Continuing the regular upward trend of previous seasons, the Wine Department has increased sales to £1,726,733($3,539,803), a rise of 17.9%. The growth in sales overseas has been most marked and in addition to the annual auction of wines in Amsterdam and Zurich, new ground was broken with a sale in Florence and one at Slane Castle, near Dublin. These, together with the fifth annual auction of rare Cape wines conducted at Nederburg on behalf of Stellenbosch Farmers' Wineries, totalled £438,756($899,450), an increase of 42.6%. Altogether over 14,200 lots have gone under the hammer.

More wine is being consigned from private sources and experts from the Department have inspected and valued many superb cellars in Belgium, Denmark, France, Germany, Holland, Italy, Spain and Switzerland. Several of these were shipped to London for subsequent sale. One of the rarest wines sold at auction, a Constantia 1791, came from British cellars, those of the Duke of Northumberland. The highest price paid was £200($410) for one half bottle.

Although the best prices are emphasised in the press, it should be remembered that a large proportion of wines sold are still at around £25 per case. At one major trade clearance sale in July, the average price per case for the 6,700 cases was about £13.50($28).

Some of the more interesting wines sold were: twelve bottles Château Cheval Blanc 1947, £1,250($2,563); twelve bottles Château Latour 1945, £1,175($2,409); one magnum Château Margaux 1870, £580($1,189); one bottle Brauneberger Juffer Beerenauslese 1937, £170($349); one bottle Château d'Yquem 1858, £665($1,363); twelve bottles Château Grillet 1971, £255($523); one double magnum Romanee Conti 1961, £380($779); twelve bottles Romanee Conti 1971, £910($1,866); one bottle Madeira 1792, £185($379); one bottle Canary *circa* 1760, £160($328); twelve bottles Dow 1890, £140($841).

Part of T. A. Layton's library of wine books, the first large collection of books sold by the Wine Department, realised £1,800($3,690). Interestingly, it proved more attractive to book dealers than to wine lovers. Among the collectors' items, rare corkscrews of quality and in good condition sold at high prices. The little interest shown in those of less quality or damaged indicates a greater sophistication among collectors. The highest price was paid for a Thomason patent type screw with a Gothic style barrel, £185($379). A King's screw with matching bone handles fetched £165($338) and an early silver folding corkscrew of unusual design with a tearshaped pull, £220($451).

Veteran and Vintage Vehicles

A 1921 Rolls-Royce Silver Ghost 40/50 h.p. tourer
Kenilworth £40,000 ($82,000). 28.VIII.78

A 1924 Morris Cowley 11.9 h.p. tourer
Donington Park £4,700 ($9,635). 21.IV.79

This car was found in Norfolk, unused since 1929, and was sold totally unrestored

A 1930 Bentley 4½-litre supercharged Le Mans replica tourer
Donington Park £34,000 ($69,700). 21.IV.79

Notes on Contributors

Geoffrey Beard is director of the Visual Arts Centre at the University of Lancaster. He has published several books on the decorative arts including *Decorative Plasterwork* (1975) and *The Work of Robert Adam* (1978). He is a friend of the Lyttelton family and wrote the guide book to Hagley Hall in 1954.

Peter Biddulph is a partner of Biddulph & Moes, stringed instrument dealers. He studied 'cello at the Royal College of Music and trained with J. & A. Beare Ltd, dealers, makers and restorers of violins.

Robert Bishop is director of the Museum of American Folk Art, New York, and associate editor of *Antique Monthly*. His publications include *Greenfield Village and Henry Ford Museum, preserving America's heritage* (1972), *American Folk Sculpture* (1974), and *The Borden Limner and his contemporaries* (1976). He is currently preparing a book on American folk painting.

Frances Buckland has been working on Sir Francis Watson's new edition of the catalogue of the furniture in the Wallace Collection, London. She is a member of the Furniture History Society and has lectured throughout the United States. Her publications include an article in the Furniture History Society Journal (1972).

Ronald Cooper studied pottery under T. S. Haile and Heber Matthews and has held teaching appointments at the colleges of art in Leeds, Willesden, and Hornsey. His publications include *The Modern Potter* (1948), *English Slipware Dishes, 1650–1850* (1968) and articles in *The Connoisseur* and *The Connoisseur Year Book*.

George Daniels is a Fellow of the Society of Antiquaries and a Fellow of the British Horological Institute. He is an expert on the history and development of the watch with special emphasis on the precision period of the late eighteenth and early nineteenth centuries. His books include *English and American Watches* (1967), *The Art of Breguet* (1975), and *Watches* (1979), written in collaboration with Cecil Clutton.

Christopher Gilbert is principal keeper of Temple Newsam House, Leeds, honorary curator of the Chippendale Society and editor of the Furniture History Society Journal. Among his publications are *The Life and Work of Thomas Chippendale* and *Furniture at Temple Newsam House and Lotherton Hall* (both 1978) and many articles on English furniture.

Brendan Gill is the Broadway drama critic of *The New Yorker* and a Fellow of the Pierpont Morgan Library. He was a long-standing friend of Benjamin Sonnenberg.

Dr Donald Harden was keeper of antiquities at the Ashmolean Museum, Oxford (1945–56), and director of the London Museum (1956–70). He has studied ancient glass for over fifty years and his publications include *Roman Glass from Karanis* (1936) and numerous articles. He is currently preparing a catalogue of pre-Roman core-formed glasses in the British Museum, London.

Dr A. S. Osley is the editor of the Quarterly Journal of the Society for Italic Handwriting. He has published several articles on calligraphy and handwriting as well as the following books: *Mercator* (1969), a monograph on the lettering of sixteenth-century Netherlandish maps, and *Luminario* (1971), the standard work on sixteenth- and seventeenth-century Italian writing books.

Jerry E. Patterson is contributing editor of *Art News* and was formerly managing editor of *Artnewsletter*. He has worked for both Sotheby's and Christie's in New York. His publications include *The City of New York, A History Illustrated from the Collections of the Museums of the City of New York* (1978).

M. M. Postnikova-Losseva is an expert at the Historical Museum, Moscow, and the leading authority on Russian silver. She has published *Russian Gold and Silver* (1967), of which she was one of four authors, and *Russian Silver, Centres and Workmasters* (1974), in addition to numerous articles in Russian journals. She has recently completed work on a book for which she has identified two thousand hitherto unrecorded marks of Russian silversmiths.

The following contributors are experts at Sotheby Parke Bernet: John Culme and Thomas Eden (in London); Brenda Auslander, John Block and Mary-Anne Martin (in New York).

Index

DATE DUE